a chance of awesome

of

awesome

how changing the way you
see changes everything

a **chance** *of* **awesome**

how changing the way you see changes everything

by **jason kotecki**

JB!RD
ink

www.jbirdink.com

Library of Congress Control Number: 2019903378
Cataloging-in-Publication Data available upon request.

ISBN 978-0-9850732-1-3 (hardcover)

ISBN 978-0-9850732-2-0 (e-book)

Books may be purchased for educational, business, or promotional use. For information on bulk purchases, please contact our team at 1-608-554-0803, or email store@escapeadulthood.com.

First Edition: July 2019

10 9 8 7 6 5 4 3 2

for St. L u *c* y

O patron saint of the blind – and of authors – may
we be inspired by your bravery and have the
courage to see with new eyes and look for the
light amidst the darkness.

[hey! check out this spread with 3D glasses!]

kotecki

the real voyage of **discovery** consists not in seeking new landscapes, but in having new eyes.

–Marcel Proust

weeds.
wishes.

kotecki

Weeds or Wishes?

"Dagnabbit! An army of weeds has taken over the yard. Better call the weed guy."

That's how most people assess a backyard populated by dandelions.

But not children. They see a thousand wishes. A thousand possibilities. A thousand flowers to give to Mom.

It's true: a backyard flush with dandelions can inspire an hour of exciting adventure for a five-year-old. The exact same backyard can also inspire an hour of expletive-laden adjectives for a fifty-year-old.

Same scene; two entirely different perspectives.

The cool thing? You get to choose. And your choice can change everything. It's the most important factor that determines the likelihood of your happiness and success. Believe it or not, most of the things we don't like about life are changeable. The tricky part is that for us to get the results we desire, the first thing that needs to change is … us.

Is it really that simple?

Actually, yes.

But that doesn't mean it's easy, thanks to something called Adultitis. My wife, Kim, and I have made it our mission to expose this terrible condition for what it is. Medically speaking, Adultitis is literally "swelling of the adult," which sums it up well. If you are walking around with a little bit too much adult within you, chances are good that your life is way more stressful than you'd like it to be, and way less fun than it could be.

A common condition occurring in people between the ages of 21 and 121, Adultitis is marked by chronic dullness, mild depression, moderate to extremely high stress levels, a general fear of change, and in some extreme cases, the inability to smile. Patients can appear aimless, discontented, and anxious about many things. Onset can be accelerated by an excess burden of bills, overwhelming responsibilities, or a boring work life. Generally, individuals with this condition are not fun to be around.

One of Adultitis's best tricks is to affect your vision. It nudges you to see dead ends as endings, problems as roadblocks, and risks as reasons to stay put.

Adultitis knows that changing the way you see, changes everything.

I'll be the first to admit that this is not an altogether novel concept. Other books have talked about the value of shifting your perspective. But then again, this is the book you have in your hands right now, which gives it a distinct advantage over all the others.

Plus, it's filled with art I created. I included the art because I think it's high time we grownups get more pictures in the books we read and because my art has a knack for getting people to see through a different lens.

Wait. Are those doughnuts sprinkling ... sprinkles? Yes.

Are the rocks in that painting of Stonehenge made of ice cream sandwiches? Yes.

Are those macarons flying saucers? Yes. And one of them is abducting a cow.

Maybe, just maybe, the way I share these ideas through my art and stories will resonate with you in a way that you need at this exact moment in time. It's my hope that even if you don't share all of my beliefs, this book will change the way you look at risk, success, failure, problems, other people, and most important, yourself.

The best way to change your life is to change the way you see.

Weeds or wishes?

a 100% Chance of Awesome

Things are rarely as they appear.

Bob Ross knew that.

The afro-sporting landscape artist who painted happy little trees often used the catchphrase "happy accidents." As an artist myself, I can attest that when errant paint drips onto my work or I accidentally smudge something I spent a long time getting just right, it can be tempting to flip out and give in to my urge to throw the canvas away. To Bob, these goofs are merely happy little accidents. Maybe that drip is the start of a tree trunk. Maybe a bush is supposed to be where that smudge is. Maybe that sky would look better in that color.

I'll admit that when I adopt that mindset of "happy accidents," I'll be danged if 99 percent of the time, my painting ends up better than it was before.

I'll also admit that reminding myself that accidents can be happy is something I still need to work on at times.

A few years ago, our basement sprang a leak. A small one, but big enough to soak part of the carpet any time a hard rain came. We bought a dehumidifier and tried keeping the gutters clear, but the battle raged on for several years. Meanwhile, Adultitis-ridden fear gremlins took up residence in my head. *What if mold is growing behind the paneling? What if it makes my kids sick? What if the repair costs $25,000? What if the mold keeps us from ever selling this house?*

Every time it rained, I got that awful feeling in the pit of my stomach.

And then one year, something remarkable happened. With the help of my dad, we tore up the carpeting (which we hated anyway) and removed the paneling to reveal the damage. Yep, there was a bit of mold and a hairline crack in the concrete. After getting rid of the damaged wood, my dad sealed the crack. We haven't had a drop of moisture since. And for a few thousand dollars, we remodeled the entire basement into a way cooler environment that includes a new studio space, where I can experiment with new media and make bigger art. The oil painting on the cover of this book would not have been made were it not for this new development.

I keep kicking myself. *Why didn't we do this sooner? Why did I let fear paralyze me for so long? How much time did I waste worrying about something that turned out to be so amazing?*

My friend Scott has a saying that Kim and I have adopted: "Now that I have this, what does this make possible?" It was originally intended to help people maximize the work they'd invested in one project by leveraging it in another. But we often use the question to frame our thought process when something bad happens. We used it the summer we spent three months in a basement with dirty, stained floors and carpet nails that needed removing. In other words, "We now have this basement in total disarray because we had to fix the water leak; what does this make possible?"

Answer: "Now we finally have a reason to create that studio space Jason's been pining for. And while we're at it, why don't we make something of that fireplace we never used by adding a cozy sitting area? And carve out a usable play zone for the kids."

Awesome opportunities are everywhere in life. Sometimes they come disguised as monsoons.

When something unexpected turns up, you have a choice: Do you dwell on the negative and listen to the fear, or do you open your eyes to the possibility that something good is just around the corner?

Becoming unexpectedly unemployed could be the spark that gets you to finally start that business.

Becoming unexpectedly pregnant could be the source of your greatest joy.

Becoming unexpectedly single could be the open door that leads to a relationship beyond your wildest dreams.

Becoming unexpectedly ill could be an opportunity to get closer to the most important people in your life.

> **These pains and troubles here are like the type that printers set. When we look at them, we see them backwards, and they seem to make no sense and have no meaning. But up there, when the Lord God prints out our life to come, we will find they make splendid reading.** –Martin Luther

Not many people love diving headlong into change. So, sometimes life comes along and kindly shoves us into it.

Did you just get pushed into a big vat of unwanted change?

Literally everything hinges upon what you do next.

Life doesn't always go as planned, but the next time a storm blows through yours, practice looking for the good things it now makes possible.

Do that, and you can expect a 100 percent chance of awesome.

SEE

with **new** eyes

kotecki

See with New Eyes

I got my first pair of glasses in eighth grade. "Oh great," I remember thinking, "Now I'm going to be one of *those* people." I figured the least I could do was select a style that would be cool.

For some reason, I thought big, brown frames with lenses the size of dinner plates fit the bill.

Since then, I've gone through quite a few frames, including the horrible clear plastic cheapos that were the best I could find in an emergency late-night mall trip. I busted lots of frames early on. At the time, I blamed my aggressive, living-on-the-edge lifestyle, but it probably had more to do with the awkwardness of puberty (good times). In a cruel twist of fate, the nasty clear plastic ones lasted the longest (good riddance, sophomore year).

I even went through a contact lens phase before ultimately deciding that glasses were easier and I got comfortable with the idea of being "one of *those* people."

One thing that hasn't changed is that I'm still near-sighted. Things far away get blurry—fast. It seems to me that glasses or no, most people are either near-sighted or far-sighted. But I'm not talking about traditional eyesight anymore.

Near-sighted people can see objects close up very clearly. Sometimes too clearly. They focus on the here and now—and all of the problems, troubles, and daily distractions that go with it—while the objects far away get fuzzy. They miss the big picture and have a difficult time dreaming big. They're the kinds of people who, when asked, have a hard time verbalizing where they see themselves in five years. They might say something like, "I'm just trying to get through the day!"

Far-sighted people, on the other hand, spend most of their time gazing into the distance. They're consumed by the next big thing: the big promotion, the larger house, the fancier car, the upcoming extravagant vacation, the next rung up on the corporate ladder. Those goals they can see clearly. Unfortunately, the little things—the wonderful, small but amazing joys right under their noses—are completely missed. These are the people Dale Carnegie was talking about when he said, "One of the most tragic things I know about human nature is that all of us tend to put off living. We are all dreaming of some magical rose garden over the horizon instead of enjoying the roses that are blooming outside our windows today."

I think all kids start out with 20/20 vision. Kids don't let the bumps and bruises that happen in life keep them from dreaming big. But they also don't get so preoccupied with future plans that they miss the neat little surprises, like a penny on the sidewalk or a ladybug crawling up a blade of grass.

We all had pretty good vision as kids. Unfortunately, most of us grew up to become "*those* people." But our vision can be corrected. We just need to look at life through some new glasses (preferably not the clear plastic ones that make you look like your face is protected by a wall of bulletproof glass).

Please keep in mind that changing your outlook will take practice.

A few years ago, it was time for new glasses (again). Besides being over four years old, my frames were one kid-bump away from total obliteration. Kim and I went to a contemporary place on State Street in Madison. I was confident I'd be able to find something unique. Two minutes into our exploration, I was not so sure. Styles change quite a bit in four years, and none of the fifteen frames the dude named Matt recommended impressed me. I *hated* most of them. I swear that this place got some of the styles directly from 1992. The clear plastic bus-windshield frames were not cool when I was a sophomore in high school, and no trendy designer is going to convince me that they're cool today.

I was prepared to walk out of there with no glasses, resolved to make friends with duct tape if my current pair bit the dust. I didn't think I was asking for too much. I merely wanted something similar to what I already had, but different.

It's kind of like how some people prefer their change: *I'll take a little bit, but not too much.*

Matt told me that my plight was a common one: You get so used to seeing your face in a particular style of glasses that everything else just looks wrong. He assured me I'd eventually find something.

After about thirty minutes of trying on over two dozen pairs of frames, I saw that he was right. I was able to narrow the field down to seven contenders. Then, after my eye exam, I picked one pair that I really liked. It's quite a departure from my old frames, but still me. And not clear plastic.

A large portion of our happiness is determined by how we decide to see things. Every once in a while, we need to change our glasses.

> **An adventure is only an inconvenience rightly considered. An inconvenience is an adventure wrongly considered.** – G. K. Chesterton

Most unpleasant circumstances that happen in our lives are truly inconveniences. Whether we view them as full-blown tragedies or unplanned adventures depends largely on what kind of glasses we are wearing.

This new perspective feels awkward and contrived when you first adopt it. After all, your old way of seeing has gotten comfortable. It feels funky at first, trying to convince yourself that losing your job or getting dumped by the person you thought was *The One* is a good thing. You might try that perspective on for a bit, but it just seems "off."

That's because you're used to seeing things the old way.

It's normal.

Don't give up; give it time.

Eventually, you'll get used to this new pair of glasses, and you'll wonder how you ever got along with those old ones.

Looking for Orcas

I've heard that God always answers prayers. Sometimes the answer is no. Sometimes He says yes in a way that merely seems like a no.

During a family vacation in the Pacific Northwest, one of the things I wanted to see was an orca.

We heard stories of a mama and her baby being spotted in Puget Sound. We kept our eyes peeled on the ferry ride to Victoria. The home we were staying in was on a bay on the Olympic Peninsula, and every wave in the distance seemed like it could be a killer whale in the process of surfacing.

We never saw one. We could have booked a sightseeing tour, but time and weather and the ages of our kids conspired against us. Maybe next time.

As I reflected on this minor disappointment, and through the act of creating this painting, something occurred to me. God knew I wanted to see an orca, but because He knows me so deeply, He also knew, before even I did, why I wanted to see one.

I had to stop and ask myself, why did I want to see an orca in the wild?

I wanted to experience God's creation in a powerful way.

I wanted to see something I'd never seen before.

I wanted to have a remarkable experience with my children.

I wanted a neat encounter with an animal.

As it turns out, I did all of those things, and I never saw one orca.

I marveled at the breathtaking vistas of Hurricane Ridge.

Our vacation home was on a beach filled with thousands of tiny crabs. I'd never seen anything like that before.

Between our mountain hike, the ferry rides, the view from the Space Needle, and a spin on Seattle's Great Wheel, there was no shortage of remarkable experiences to be shared with my kids.

And feeding some high-spirited harbor seals in Victoria with a $2 bag of fish heads was a neat animal encounter.

Time and time again in my life, I didn't get what I asked for.

I thought I wanted to marry a brunette. God knew that what I really wanted was a beautiful, smart, and thoughtful wife who believed in me. He also made her blonde.

I wanted to use my art to make a living and shine light and goodness in the world. I asked for it in the form of being a professional syndicated cartoonist. That never materialized. But here I am, using my art to make a living and shine light and goodness in the world in a way that I never could have imagined but I am excited to say is even better.

Sometimes we miss the answer to our prayers because we're looking in the wrong place.

Space Invaders

If you are lucky, you are old enough to remember the Atari video game system, which was a far cry from the advanced graphics we see in games today. And it had only one button!

One of the most popular games was called Space Invaders, which I have featured prominently in this painting. It has a simple concept: you try to shoot as many aliens as you can as they descend down your screen. As the game continues, the aliens plummet at an ever-increasing speed. If they reach the bottom, the alien invasion is successful and the game ends.

To me, this is a great metaphor for Adultitis. Although I wish there were a magic potion or miracle cure that could end this terrible condition once and for all, there just isn't. Adultitis is always coming after us, just like those aliens. You can blast down a whole screen by going to Disney World, but on your first day back to work, another wave is ready to strike.

The key, I think, is to look at fighting Adultitis as a game. It's most deadly when it hides in the shadows, convincing you to take yourself too seriously and getting you to focus on the negative. But if you notice where it tries to sabotage you, and laugh at its advances, you can diffuse its power.

Our family has had great fun in acknowledging when Adultitis has gained the upper hand, and we encourage one another to fight back. Extreme cases call for an ice cream run or a spontaneous dance party in the kitchen.

My dad is fond of saying, "Everything happens for a reason."

Well, I make it a game to try to figure out the reason. Any time something bad happens, I try to start thinking about what good could come from it. (As I shared in my leaky-basement story, sometimes it takes me a while to get there.) What if you looked at the challenges you face as being like any other game?

- Instead of looking at hitting your sales numbers as a life-or-death situation, make it into a game.

- Instead of worrying about not getting everything done today, make it into a game.

- Instead of stressing out over how you'll ever be able to conform to the new regulations in your industry, make it into a game.

Instead of acting like your current challenge is something found in the bad-tasting-medicine aisle, see if you can mentally repackage it in primary colors and take it from the toy section. Breathe. Smile. Have some fun with it. By looking at it as a game and clearing your mind of the useless worst-case scenarios, you'll be MORE likely to notice the people, opportunities, and ideas you'll need to win.

You may believe that the stakes are much higher now compared to a silly game of Space Invaders. But are they really? With VERY few exceptions, the truth is that our fear of failure is worse than the consequences that come from actually failing. Sure, the project very well might flop, your efforts might go to waste, or someone may laugh at you. You could get rejected, dejected, or fired.

Sometimes, like the aliens, Adultitis advances past your defenses and wins the day.

But you know what? The good news is that you can hit Reset and start again. Life WILL go on. It will be okay. You will be able to pick yourself up, dust yourself off, and get ready for the new—even better!—opportunity right around the corner.

Are you game?

Get Up Faster

I once had the good fortune to hear a woman named Bonnie St. John give a speech. Bonnie is a downhill skier. Oh yeah, and she has only one leg.

She talked about competing in a Paralympic event. She made it to the medal round, but during a speedy run down the mountain, she slipped and fell. Emotions of all sorts swelled up within her. Frustrated, angry, and heartbroken, she sat in the snow, knowing that she had cost herself the gold. Eventually, dejectedly, she got back up and headed toward the finish line to complete the race.

She didn't win.

But later she found out that the gold medal winner had also fallen during her run. The secret to her victory?

She got up faster.

Life is hard sometimes. People can be jerks. That's just how it goes. The worst things often happen when you're right in the middle of striving for something great; they're the circumstances that test your mettle to see what you're made of. You can't always control the things that happen to you, but you can ALWAYS control how you react to them.

Life has no shortage of opportunities for you to practice getting up faster.

Like the day I sold my first oil painting at the Escape Adulthood Summit. I had only recently begun offering originals for sale, and I was elated.

I proudly added a "sold" sign to the canvas, a badge of honor that would be on display for the rest of the event.

Later that day, I felt a disturbance in the Force. Someone had inadvertently knocked over a few of the paintings. I calmly walked over to the scene, planning to reset them on their easels. No biggie. But my gut turned upside down when I grabbed the sold painting and discovered a huge gash in the canvas. It had fallen onto—and was impaled by—a smaller easel below. The hole created by the fall made the painting look like it had come face-to-face with an angry art critic named Freddy Krueger.

I was sick—mostly for my friend Jessica, who had bought the painting and was excited to have it. I groped for something to say. "Ha ha, this makes it more unique now?" I said. "This comes with a great story, right?" I tried to think of a

solution to save the day, but I just couldn't. Only days earlier, I'd read that when artists want to be rid of a piece that they don't like or hasn't sold, the surest way to do the job is to slash the canvas with a knife. Yep. This felt unfixable. I didn't see any good solution, short of refunding her money and mourning the loss of my short-lived first sale.

But a short time later, Jessica turned the tide with a suggestion. She noted that many of my other pieces incorporated words in a collage style, while this one didn't. "Could you maybe add some words to it that would cover up the hole?"

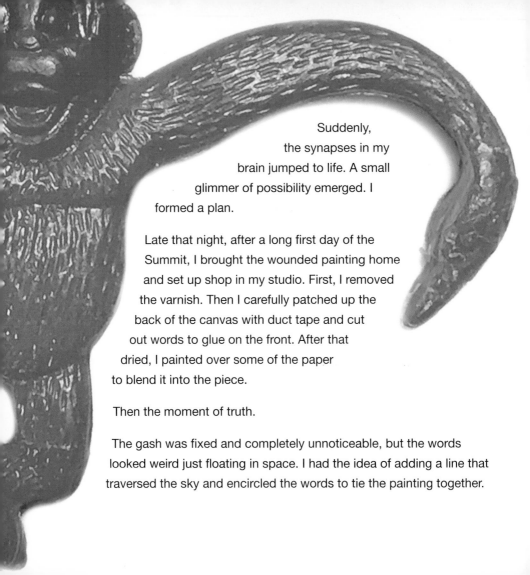

Suddenly, the synapses in my brain jumped to life. A small glimmer of possibility emerged. I formed a plan.

Late that night, after a long first day of the Summit, I brought the wounded painting home and set up shop in my studio. First, I removed the varnish. Then I carefully patched up the back of the canvas with duct tape and cut out words to glue on the front. After that dried, I painted over some of the paper to blend it into the piece.

Then the moment of truth.

The gash was fixed and completely unnoticeable, but the words looked weird just floating in space. I had the idea of adding a line that traversed the sky and encircled the words to tie the painting together.

It was risky. I'd have to use an oil paint stick, with no good way to erase it without potentially ruining the entire painting. I had one shot to get it right. After discussing it with Kim, I went for it.

A few minutes later, just after midnight, I emerged from my laboratory with the resurrected painting. I had nailed it.

I was excited to arrive early for day two of the Summit so I could replace the fixed painting before everyone else arrived and surprise Jess. It was fun to see her do a double-take when she noticed the change. She told me she had been an art major for a brief time and suggested that the composition of the "new" painting was even better than that of the first one. She was right. It *was* a better painting in every way.

One that *did* come with a great story.

A big theme of this book is fostering the habit of looking at potential disasters as possibilities. I'll admit that I was in too much shock at first to figure out any way to turn the gashed painting into a positive. Despite all my good intentions to look at unfortunate developments as "happy accidents," there didn't seem to be anything happy about this one.

It would have been easy to dismiss any fixes: "That'll never work! It's ruined, and that's that!" Fortunately, as hopeless as I felt, I was still open to the possibility of a happy ending. Jessica's suggestion was the nudge I needed to find it.

Silver linings are easier to spot when you're looking for them.

Bad things happen. Unexpected, unwelcome, unfortunate, unsettling things that make us sad, frustrated, and angry. (Sometimes all of the above.) And as humans, we find it hard to adopt a bulletproof positive attitude and bounce back immediately from these setbacks. That's okay. It's healthy to sulk, vent, and grieve for a spell. But it's also healthy to be open to the idea that something good can come out of this terrible turn of events.

Sometimes that terrible turn of events delivers something that leaves us better off than we were before.

When life slashes your canvas, take a time-out. Get some perspective.

And practice getting up faster.

enjoy the woo

Enjoy the Woo

I think it's safe to assume that physically, plunging down the first drop on a roller coaster feels a lot like riding a runaway train hurtling off a cliff. (Admittedly, I've never actually experienced the latter.) Even though our brains know the ultimate outcome of each event, both experiences will cause us to scream like that thief in *Home Alone* who had the tarantula walk on his face.

I'm an eternal optimist (I grew up a Cubs fan, after all), but also a bit of a worrier. When an unexpected expense comes up, or the bank account looks smaller than it should, or an abnormality on a medical test pops up, I'm only a hop, skip, and jump away from pushing the panic button.

It's in those moments that my life feels like a runaway train and I'm racing toward certain doom. My fear is something terrible and my faith is tested.

And yet, so far, disaster is always avoided. The car rights itself; the path levels out; God provides. It's not that bad things never happen, but that they somehow give way to something good.

What I try to do is own the metaphor of the roller coaster. When you get on a roller coaster, you know that you are safe. The ride has been carefully designed and the passengers return unscathed. Although the giant drops and corkscrews elicit bloodcurdling screams, you know that you are not in any real danger, and that knowledge is what makes the ride so thrilling and enjoyable. The terror becomes fun—a stress release of sorts—and you can fully give yourself over to the experience.

That's how I want to look at life. Instead of fearing the worst and losing faith every time I encounter a perilous situation, I want to know in my deepest being that things will always work out in the end, even if I can't imagine how. That knowledge will allow me to shift the way I look at things. I can give myself over to the thrill of the ride, feeling the rush at the core of my soul, fully expecting that my car will end up safely back at the station. I can watch and appreciate what God is doing in my life, rather than fear that I have been completely abandoned.

That's how I think God designed life to be: a thrill ride. A series of exciting ups and downs and unforeseen twists that's over too quickly. One that finds us rolling into the station called Heaven at the end of our ride, excitedly saying, "That was AWESOME! I wanna do it again!"

I suppose it is natural to want to go through life via the smooth road. No bumps or dips, no sharp turns or precipitous drops. We crave comfort.

And yet how boring would that be?

Fortunately (or unfortunately, depending on your perspective), life doesn't work that way. There are ups and downs and moments fraught with terror.

It basically comes down to this: Do I believe that I am on a runaway train hurtling toward a broken bridge, or am I on a roller coaster at the greatest amusement park in existence?

Yes, it is a choice.

I choose the roller coaster.

You?

BEE
OPTIMISTIC

kotecki

Bee Optimistic

One of the most challenging skills to master in baseball is hitting a curve ball, especially a nasty one. When I played ball in high school, we practiced with Wiffle balls to try to get used to the spin and trajectory of the pitch. Practice was nothing compared to the real thing, though.

In the heat of the battle, the eyes of the spectators are on you. If a strong, tall lefty unleashes a big bender, your mind suddenly goes into decision-by-committee mode. Your upper body lunges forward, eager to pounce on an offering that is slower than a fastball. Your knees buckle, as if to say, "Mayday! Mayday! It's coming right for us!" Meanwhile, your feet turn into cement blocks, paralyzed by indecision.

Best-case scenario, you take a good cut at the ball, maybe even put it into play. Worst-case scenario, you look like a drunk gardener with arms made of spaghetti, trying to whack a wasp with a rake.

No matter who you are, the game of life throws you a lot of curveballs.

Speaking of which…

The phone call came minutes after I walked off stage after a speaking program. It was my wife, Kim, alerting me that my dad wanted to arrange an urgent family meeting for the next day. As he has a bit of a history of overhyping things, I couldn't help but wonder about the true importance of this meeting, especially since the following day was the only day I'd be home in the span of a week.

A call back to Dad confirmed that the situation was serious, and he was adamant that he didn't want to tell us the news by phone.

Gulp.

And so began a twenty-four-hour waiting period in which the only thing to do was entertain worst-case scenarios and pray that somehow things would work out. I spent the rest of the evening trying to get my mind off the situation, suddenly empathizing with everyone who has ever had to wait for a diagnosis. No matter how dire the news, there is a certain peace in knowing what you're dealing with. But the waiting (and the not knowing) is torture.

The next day, I convened with my brothers and our wives at my youngest brother's house. While waiting for my parents to arrive, we ate some pumpkin desserts my sister-in-law had whipped up, as if the sweetness would some-how counteract the sour news we all anticipated.

A million years later, my parents' car pulled into the driveway. My mom looked like she was wearing a white sweatshirt with the hood pulled over her head. While teenagers have perfected this look, I was not about to assume that my sixty-year-old mother had suddenly gotten hip. This did not look good and seemed to confirm our suspicions that this terrible news was centered around her.

As my parents got out of the car, we could see that Mom was not, in fact, wearing a hoodie. She was wearing a beekeeping costume.

Yep, you read that right. *A beekeeping costume.*

Meanwhile—get this!—my dad emerged dressed head-to-toe as a bee.

What the ... ?!

We were all confused as could be, but still secretly wished that this ridiculous-ness was a sign that the news was not as bad as we feared. Maybe this was just "Dad being Dad."

We exchanged hugs, and my parents seemed to be in good spirits. I wanted to exhale, assured that my worst fears were just the byproduct of an overactive imagination. I glanced at the uncertain smiles on the faces of my family members and hoped that we'd soon be pleasantly surprised with positive news that we never saw coming.

Then my dad set up a makeshift cardboard lectern in the living room and pulled out a homemade sign, made on loose-leaf paper, that he taped to the front. It read, "Stuff Happens." Below that was a smiley face next to a frowny face. The frowny face had an "x" through it. Hope quickly evaporated from the room. It felt hard to breathe. We braced for the worst.

All eyes were fixed on my dad, who started the meeting by reminding us how many tough challenges we'd gotten through as a family over the years. On and on he went, testing the patience of his children and his wife, who was sitting in a chair on the opposite side of the room.

Finally, this man, my father, the one dressed up like a bee, bravely told us that he had cancer.

At first, my heart plummeted into my stomach. But as he explained the kind of cancer he had (prostate), shared that they had caught it early, and told us how high the survival rate is, hope slowly returned. He said that he and Mom had resolved to be positive and optimistic, which is why they decided to lighten the mood by coming dressed in the Halloween costumes they had worn at a party the night before.

He said, "We hoped it would take the *sting* out of the news we had to share."

I am not even kidding.

We eventually learned that my parents had worn the costumes for the entire two-hour drive up to Wisconsin, a trip that included a stop to pump gas as well as a visit to the Burger King drive-thru.

As the mood lightened and we followed my parents' optimistic lead, all I could think was, *I bet no one in the history of ever has told his family that he had cancer while wearing a bee costume.*

But that's exactly what my dad did.

He is a shining example of how even though we can't control what life throws at us, we can control whether we'll strike out or swing for the fences.

My dad came through the other side, prostate-free but filled with perspective and gratitude. Since then, my mom has won her own battle with cancer. Both parents tell me they feel like they won the lottery. In their regular visits to the Cancer Treatment Center of America, they have encountered people who were in much tougher fights. In addition, through our work with the Make-A-Wish Foundation, Kim and I have met a lot of beautiful families, all of whom have been dealt hands I wouldn't wish on my worst enemy. It's impossible not to want to help.

But how do you help fight cancer? It's so big and scary and ugly, and we are so small.

One of the habits my dad has is handing out Bee pins.

Shortly after the big meeting with the bee and his keeper, I made a painting for my dad featuring his favorite insect and the message "Bee Optimistic." It was equal parts encourage-ment and tribute to his positivity. He asked if I could make him a "Bee Optimis-tic" pin that he could wear every day. I did, and he does.

Since then, he's given out hundreds of pins. Like a volunteer at a marathon handing out water to the runners, he gives a pin to anyone he meets who has been touched by the shadow of cancer.

Fighting cancer is a hard race. Faith and hope are the water you need to keep going. When my dad hands out the Bee pins, he is handing out hope. Although the action is small, the impact is huge.

Life will throw you curveballs. No matter who you are, people are watching, be it your kids, your employees, or your biggest fans. I guess the lesson is that if you keep a childlike spirit and focus on maintaining a sense of optimism, you'll have a better chance of not looking like a drunk gardener with spaghetti arms.

It always helps to bee optimistic.

Mind Your Own Monkeys

Since 94 percent of the population suffers from at least a mild form of Adultitis, odds are that anyone with a job has to work with someone infected with this vile disease. Maybe it's a co-worker or a client or—yikes!—the boss. Sometimes the people I chat with after my speaking programs will confess to being married to someone with a full-blown case of Adultitis.

So the question, of course, is, *how do I fix someone who has it?*

Unfortunately, the truth is … you don't.

I am a professional speaker. Most speakers I know started their careers with the hope of making a difference and changing lives. I certainly did.

If you do it long enough, though, you'll likely come across some uplifting statistic that informs you that your audience will probably forget almost everything you said the minute they walk out the door. Eventually you will realize that you do not have any power whatsoever to change someone's life. Entertain, sure. Inspire, maybe. But change? That's up to them, not you. (News flash: this handy rule also applies to any husbands, wives, parents, and teachers who may be reading.)

It's hard not to feel like you're a professional exerciser in futility.

The thing is, the more quickly you accept this reality, the better speaker you become.

When you are not worried about whether you will get a standing ovation, or about the lady who ducked out the back, or about the guy in the front row with crossed arms who seems like he'd rather be shaving rabid goats with a broken razor, you will be able to focus more on being your authentic, true self, allowing your message to land where it will.

And THEN you might make some sort of difference for someone.

You might not make your living from being on stage, but wherever you work, the principle is the same. When you're dealing with people who have Adultitis, there is only so much you can do. This is it:

1) Be a good example. Take yourself lightly. Live your life cheerfully, with humor and joyful anticipation. In the best-case scenario, people will see and be inspired by your approach to life, and a little of that will rub off on them. Maybe they'll even ask for your secret, and then you can help them on the road to recovery.

2) Send kindness. If your example alone doesn't make a dent, you should put their office supplies or car keys into Jell-O molds. (Just kidding.) (Not really.) But do keep in mind that everyone is fighting a hard battle. Maybe they're tired from working overtime to pay for insurance. Maybe their dog just died. Maybe you could try sending them flowers or a box of cookies because maybe they just need someone to notice them and be kind to them.

3) Limit exposure. If you're still running into a brick wall of Adultitis, your only other option is to ignore those people and do your best to limit your exposure to them. You don't have to be mean about it; you just have to be intentional.

Depending on the relationship, you might consider deleting them from your life. Harsh, I know, but life is too short to have the joy sucked out of you by someone with advanced Adultitis.

"Whoa, buddy," you may be thinking. "That's a little extreme. And it's not exactly gonna work. This is my spouse you're talking about," or, "I can't exactly fire my idiot co-worker." If extracting yourself from the situation is not an option, you should make it a priority to surround yourself with people who are relatively Adultitis-free. These relationships will help bolster your energy levels and serve as a force field against the Adultitis-ridden zombies in your life.

Is it an ideal solution? No, but it's reality.

Yes, you can grumble about the things you can't control, and complain about the mess the people in charge have made. You can throw your hands up and declare that there's nothing you can do about it. It may actually be true that there are things you have no power to change. But that doesn't let you off the hook.

You are the ringmaster of *your* circus and *your* monkeys. Focus on the things you can control: your attitude, your actions, and the people you choose to spend most of your time with. Let go of the things you can't control.

You may not be able to make someone change, but it's always possible to make a difference. If you're disappointed or frustrated by your spouse, your job, your boss, or your kids, you always have the option of waiting for them to improve. Or you can instigate a small rebellion and spark a magical turnaround by changing the way you look at them and the way you act around them.

Just don't be surprised if what changes is *you.*

"attitude is
the mind's
paintbrush.
it can color
any situation.

–Barbara Johnson

duck   duck

Duck, Duck, Goose

Remember that childhood game Duck, Duck, Goose? (Special shout-out to my weird friends from Minnesota who call it Duck, Duck, Gray Duck.) Whatever you call it, a bunch of kids sit in a circle. One kid, referred to as "it," walks the circumference, tapping the seated kids one by one, saying, "Duck, duck," until finally tapping one and saying, "Goose!" Then that kid has to chase and tag "it" before "it" makes it back around the circle to the open space.

During the game, as "it" makes his or her way around the circle, all of the other children are usually pretty still. A little anxious, perhaps, but it's definitely the calm before the storm until "Goose!" is called and all heck breaks loose.

These days, life is too much like the second part—too much running around like chickens (or ducks) with our heads cut off. Not surprisingly, this makes it awfully hard to see clearly. We need more time to be still.

Somehow our society got the idea that "busy" is good and admirable, a sign that we're successful. Even our vacations are busy. (Gotta do and see everything you possibly can!) We are afraid of the quiet. We listen to music when we jog, keep the radio on during our commutes, and leave the TV on while we do household chores.

If changing the way we see can change the direction of our lives, then perhaps it makes sense to try to see as clearly as we can.

And the best way to do that is to s l o w d o w n.

Corita Kent was one of America's most celebrated serigraph artists. She was also a Catholic nun who delivered messages of hope and joy to a troubled world. In *Learning By Heart*, a book about her teachings, she says, "There are two ways of looking—slow looking and fast looking. Slow looking is best done alone."

As an art professor at Immaculate Heart College in Los Angeles, she gave her students empty 35mm slide holders that she called "finders." She instructed her students to take their finders to busy gathering places and look at the world through the finders for half an hour. Kent explained that the finder "does the same thing as the camera lens or viewfinder. It helps take things out of context, allows us to see for the sake of seeing, and enhances our quick-looking and decision-making skills." This simple practice helped her students to slow down and see with new eyes, revealing the beauty in small parts of the world around them.

> **One purpose of art is to alert people to things they might have missed.** –Corita Kent

Too often, we're like jars of muddy water. When we're busy and in constant motion, our vision can get cloudy. But if we take the time to sit for a bit, the dirt settles and life gets clearer. You can shake the jar as forcefully as you want (work harder), but until you STOP, you won't be able to see clearly, thereby allowing yourself to work smarter.

Again, we can learn a lot from children. In her article "Quest for Quietness," Ruth Liew writes:

> *Young children like a quiet hideaway place. Sometimes this place is in a discarded box or a space under the stairs or a wardrobe. Some children crawl under the bed or the dining table and imagine they are in another, faraway place.*
>
> *When children are given free time, they tend to achieve more because they are not stressed by demands. I remember watching a precocious three-year-old who seemed a little "lost" in her nursery school. While the other children were in their respective classrooms, she would lie down on a large cushion and perform her own soliloquies.*
>
> *She would say, "I don't know why I don't have any friends. I like them but they don't like me. What shall I do?" After uttering those words, she got up and went to meet her peers in the next room. She had worked it all out by herself. Children discover their inner selves when they retreat from the hustle and bustle of daily life.*

When life gets muddy and out of control, the secret to clarity is to find a secret hideaway place, slow down, and be still.

you might not need more exposure to the new. instead, it might pay to re-see what's already around you.

–Seth Godin

Willing to Relocate

When Kim and I decided to move to Madison, Wisconsin, after we got married, neither of us had jobs, or job prospects for that matter. I'm sure some people thought we were crazy.

Kim and I didn't *have* to leave our hometowns in Illinois. They were fine and offered opportunity. But we wanted an adventure to call our own and suspected that the life we wanted to live would require a change of scenery. And so we were willing to relocate.

We had to leave behind that which was familiar in order to grow into who we were meant to become. We picked Madison, but in our case, the need to move away from our comfort zone was more important than the actual location itself.

Sometimes we have to be willing to relocate in order to make our dreams come true. Of course, that might mean moving across town or across the country.

Or it might mean moving into a different group of friends.

It might mean moving from where our customers are today to where they will be tomorrow.

It might mean moving into a new way of seeing ourselves, perhaps from the role of victim to that of victor.

When I was a brand new speaker, Kim and I helped form a mastermind group with a few of our peers, talented people in similar stages of their businesses as we were. We had the harebrained idea to invite Robert into our group. Robert was a true pro whom we all looked up to. He'd been speaking for years and had a thriving business. We never thought he'd actually say yes.

He did.

The thing that impressed me most about Robert was his openness to new ideas. He shared hard-earned lessons, but never paraded the fact that he was further along than the rest of us. He looked at us as true peers. He was always curious. He regularly asked us for our opinions and was eager to try out our suggestions.

I remember thinking that when I grew up and got really successful, I wanted to be like Robert.

Here's the thing. He wasn't patronizing us; he was smart. He knew that in order to grow his business and get better as a speaker, he couldn't stay where he was. He had to be willing to relocate.

Sadly, the reason he stood out is that his attitude is rare. I've seen many speakers—and organizations for that matter—slowly fade into oblivion and irrelevance because pride held them back. They already knew it all. They weren't open to a new path.

Robert was successful. But he wasn't about to settle.

If you are not satisfied with your life as it is now, you have to be willing to relocate from where you are now to where you want to be.

If you want to experience the summit, you have to say goodbye to sea level.

Draw Upside Down

When I'm working on a painting, I have to step back from time to time. I have to literally stop the activity of painting and be still before the work. Otherwise, I can't see the painting through the brushstrokes.

You might think that pausing slows down the process. What it really does is help me make better paintings.

If I don't step away every so often, I'm liable to get stuck overdoing part of the painting and end up ruining the whole thing. Giving myself some distance helps me notice certain aspects that I can't see when I'm up close. I can examine the overall composition, observe the balance of color, and see if the values are working well together. If I get a feeling that something's not quite right, stepping back and taking a look at the big picture can help me pinpoint the problem.

Sometimes, I simply step back to admire what I've created. One of my favorite parts of making art is the moment of pride I have when something

turns out so well that I can hardly believe I did it.

The same is true of our lives. We need to take time every once in a while to step back and see what we're creating. Too often, we get stuck in survival mode, busily checking off one task after another, rarely coming up for a breather for fear that we'll fall farther behind—or worse, be faced with the realization that our efforts have been misplaced and we've been focusing on the wrong things.

> **Nothing is less productive than to make more efficient what should not be done at all.**
> —Peter Drucker

This is exactly what Adultitis wants: for you to stay busy, distracted, and more likely to veer off course.

So if you get a sense that something about your life is not quite right, take some time to step away for a bit. Go for a long walk, sit for an hour in a quiet church, or take a day off and unplug from technology.

Look for areas in your life that you might be neglecting, and for those that you might be spending too much time on. But also spend some time in gratitude for the blessings you have, and applaud yourself for the little things you've done well. Instead of focusing on where you fall short, appreciate how far you've come.

There is a reason every major world religion is so big on taking a Sabbath. Stopping might make you feel less productive. But what it really does is help you make life better.

If we busy ourselves with brushstrokes, we risk losing sight of the big picture. Stopping to step back and examine our lives makes it less likely that we'll end up with a mess on our hands, and more likely that we'll create something spectacular.

Whenever I draw a portrait, I have another technique I employ—one my wife thinks is weird. After I get the major shapes and outlines blocked in, I turn my reference photos and artwork upside down. Then I keep drawing.

The reason I do this is that inevitably, during the course of creating a portrait, I get to a point where something seems "off." Because I think I know what a nose is supposed to look like, I get lazy and draw what I "know," not what I see. Turning my paper upside down tricks my brain into forgetting that this is a nose so I can see it for what it really is: areas of shape and form. In order to nail the likeness, I need to focus on values and lines, not noses and eyes. I need to rely on reality, not assumptions.

This simple trick immediately allows me to see where I went wrong so I can make the necessary adjustments.

The cool thing is that you can use this same strategy to make your life, relationships, or business better. Sometimes it's not new ideas we need, but a new perspective.

Spend the day doing the work of a frontline employee.

Explore how people do what you do in other countries around the world.

Or maybe you and your spouse could swap chores for a few days.

The point is to let go of your assumptions and experience something as it really is. As Isaac Asimov said, "Your assumptions are your windows on the world. Scrub them off every once in a while, or the light won't come in."

If something you care about (such as your business, a relationship, or a project at work) isn't quite turning out the way you'd like, give yourself a new perspective and a shot at a breakthrough.

Turn things upside down.

imagination can take YOU ANYWHERE

Art vs. Science

In my family, when I was growing up, I was always the art guy. Today, I make a living painting pictures, telling stories, and writing books. My younger brother Dan was the science guy. He now works for a cancer hospital, analyzing and improving systems, or something structured and boring like that. I always saw us as complete opposites, which is how I think most people see art and science.

Yes, my brother and I are different, but I was also decent at math and enjoyed doing experiments in chemistry class. Meanwhile, he had a decent drawing talent that went under the radar. Today he collects Pearl Jam posters because he appreciates the art.

For many years, I was so locked into looking at the differences between us that I never noticed the connections.

Artists are thought of as free-spirited, open-ended, and subjective. Scientists are often viewed as analytical, precise, and objective. But science is not cold, rigid, and unfeeling. Art is not some frivolous, fluffy extra. Believe it or not, they are connected.

Curiosity and imagination are the parents of both art and science.

The same curiosity and imagination that are present when an artist creates a new play, sculpture, or piece of music are present in the best scientists as well. We imagine space travel, and curiosity asks, "How can we make that happen?" We imagine a world without cancer, and curiosity asks, "What hasn't been tried on this particular strain?" Curiosity asks, "How can we become more energy independent?" and our imagination gets to work on thinking up a whole bunch of possible solutions, ranging from the farfetched to the less so. Sometimes solutions are hidden within an idea that seems completely preposterous.

The painting that opened this chapter was inspired by my first trip to Vancouver and by a quote often attributed (likely incorrectly) to Albert Einstein: "Logic will get you from A to B. Imagination will take you everywhere."

Imagination is often seen as a peculiar skillset of children and the pastime of daydreamers—mildly amusing, but hardly practical for a self-respecting adult. Too often, our imaginations fade as we grow older. We stop asking questions and dreaming big. We reward the rule-followers. We search for and obediently follow the best practices.

But in a changing world, what worked before will not get us to where we need to go. There is no roadmap. No formula. No step-by-step manual to help us succeed tomorrow.

The well-worn paths we're used to treading now only lead us astray, to a world that no longer exists.

So what now?

We must stop looking at science and art as opposing forces.

We need to realize that we are all artists. Working in paint, charcoal, or clay is not required. And likewise, we are all scientists, even if we don't wear lab coats.

If you feel stuck or have a sneaking suspicion that things could be better in your life, your relationships, or your organization, you are right. The way forward is to imagine a better reality, the future you wish to create. And then you tinker your way there by trying things that might not work and using what you learn to guide your next steps—even small steps—forward.

Imagination. It's not just a plaything for children.

Dust yours off. It can take you to some amazing places.

"the only limits are, as always, those of vision.

–James Broughton

this ai N'T KANSAS

This Ain't Kansas

As dissimilar as they may appear on the surface, rural Midwestern farmers and rural Asian farmers have some things in common. One of the most important is a deep respect for tradition. This value provides a sense of stability and helps people pass on their hard-earned wisdom to future generations.

But I believe we must also have an openness to new things—not so that we will abandon our ideals, but so that we can experience a much richer life. It's like the difference between black-and-white and full color; think of the wonderment on Dorothy's face as she emerges from her tornado-tossed, sepia-toned house into the Technicolor landscape in the 1939 version of *The Wizard of Oz*.

Indeed, doing things the way you've always done them, and surrounding yourself with the same people, places, and opinions that you've always been exposed to, is a good way to live life in grayscale.

I made this piece as a reminder that sometimes we need to break free from what's expected. Mashups of east and west, urban and rural, liberal and conservative, old and new are what make life more interesting.

How does one opt for a more Technicolor life? Simple: Take a break from your traditions and routines.

Read a magazine or watch a documentary on a subject you know nothing about. Order food you've never tasted before. Take a new form of transportation to work for a week. Have a conversation with someone who holds an opposite point of view (without trying to convince them they're wrong).

This openness to new ideas, perspectives, and ways of doing things is a key to unlocking opportunities that can change your life.

I have struggled the past few years with trying to find my place. I have been a member of the National Speakers Association for over a decade now and it has served me well. I have made wonderful friends and have learned a lot about growing a successful speaking business. But in recent years, I've had a hard time finding relevant examples to model my business after. You see, I have this art thing that I do, which is unique among the speakers I've encountered. Even the ones who incorporate art into their offerings do so in a way that's totally different from the direction I want to head in.

And so I have spent the better part of the last two years seeking out art-centered business models. I have tried to learn as much as I can from other successful artists. I've learned a lot, but it turns out that most of these artists aren't so keen on the whole "speaking in front of large crowds" thing.

I was frustrated by my failure to find someone who has already done what I am trying to do. Someone who has a roadmap I can follow.

Until I finally figured out that there is magic in the mashup.

It's the combination of two seemingly unrelated skills—public speaking and making art—that gives me my edge and helps me stand out. Borrowing the best of what I've learned from great speakers and successful artists, while mixing in my own unique quirks and talents, has been a game changer for me.

If you've been feeling paralyzed by the belief that things have to go a certain way, or if you've felt like a square peg trying to force yourself into a round hole, or if life just feels a tad too gray, it might be time to mix in some new ideas, experiences, and assumptions.

And watch your world change.

the **best**
Adventure s
follow **no** MAPS

koлecki

Best Practices Are for the Birds

I live in Wisconsin. As you may have heard, we eat cheese at every meal.

So naturally, one day my wife was making grilled cheese sandwiches for lunch. My then four-year-old daughter Lucy was eager to help. Kim handed her a butter knife and invited her to butter the bread, with one simple instruction: "Just butter one side."

So she did.

I'm not going to argue that this is the best way to make a grilled cheese sandwich (pretty sure it's not), but I will argue that very few of us would have even considered this an option.

That's the problem with us grownups. We are so enamored with best practices, we don't even consider whether better ones could exist.

Best practices are for the birds.

Remember when your mom asked you if you'd jump off a bridge if all your friends did? Nowadays you could get away with saying "yes" if you explained that jumping off the bridge was a "best practice."

Look, I'm all for seeking wisdom and learning from others who are experts, but I'm beginning to see "best practices" morph into a fancy way of saying, "Tell me what to do so I don't have to think." Relying on them has become just as much a way of hiding as it has a tool for improvement. After all, no one ever got fired for following a best practice.

Best practices are the equivalent of paint-by-numbers: "Color these sections exactly the way we tell you and you'll end up with a pretty picture that looks exactly like this."

The problem is, they don't hang paint-by-numbers in the Louvre.

Innovation is a sexy buzzword these days. Everyone wants to be seen as innovative, but you can't be innovative if you're busy following best practices. Doing the same thing as everyone else is the *opposite* of innovation. If you want to be innovative, you have to find *better* practices. The only way to do that is to try doing something different. Of course, it might not work. But … what if it does?

Not so long ago, one company made it to the top by establishing and following these best practices:

1) Secure an expensive physical site in an easily accessible location near lots of people.

2) Buy tons of copies of the newest and most popular movies, while ignoring the niche films and obscure documentaries.

3) Charge late fees to ensure that customers return your movies on time.

Not so best anymore, eh?

You can follow best practices or you can be innovative, but you can't do both.

The head-fake here is that this little rant seems to be all about business, but it's really not. It's about life. The map is there for you if you want it. Many people follow this one:

1) Go to school to earn a degree in a field that has a high demand and a promising future.

2) Use that degree to secure a job with great benefits, a 401(k), and room for advancement.

3) Hate your job for years until you can finally retire and live off that 401(k) you worked so hard to earn.

You can navigate your career, raise your kids, spend your free time, direct your education, plan your wedding, celebrate holidays, run your campaign, decorate your home, or manage your finances according to best practices. If you want your life to look like everyone else's, by all means look around, watch what everyone else is doing, and do that. Frankly, that's what many people want.

But if you are reading this, I suspect you want something more than for your life to look like a boring old paint-by-number exactly like everyone else's. In order to get that something more, you have to ignore the map and head off for parts unknown. That's what "escaping adulthood" is all about.

The scary part is not that you don't know where to head. (There may be a good chance that deep down, you actually do.)

Making the decision to start: that's the scary part. It's also the beginning of a great adventure.

one more thing...

After one of my speaking engagements, I was talking to a woman who told me about an unusual bug her car possessed. She explained that sometimes, while she was driving with her kids in tow, her car would suddenly take on a life of its own. There was nothing she could do to control the direction

it was headed in. No matter how hard she jerked the steering wheel left, if the vehicle wanted to turn right, it went right, with the kids erupting into a frenzy of excited, anxious squeals. The woman explained that there didn't seem to be any rhyme or reason for the erratic behavior. Sometimes it would happen after school, other times after a long day of chores.

The most interesting part of the story is where the car ended up. Without exception, the destination was always an ice cream shop. At that point, the beleaguered mom admitted, it only seemed right to order a few cones.

After doing a dash of research, I've discovered that this isn't a *flaw* in this woman's vehicle, but a *feature*. And—surprise!—it comes standard in every single car, truck, van, and SUV, including mine.

And yours.

Sometimes days go south and life is such that it calls for a deviation from the current script. I'm not saying ice cream is the answer for everything, but it does have some magical powers to turn a day around.

Of course, this isn't really about ice cream. **The point is that sometimes a day filled with left turns needs a perfectly timed right one.**

Good thing we have the technology at our disposal to help us out with that.

Hippoposterous

This is a tiny hippo in a bowl of Froot Loops. Or is it a normal-sized hippo in a giant bowl of Froot Loops?

I don't remember.

Either way, it's preposterous.

Most serious people don't have time for the preposterous. They have much more important things to concern themselves with. Of course, there's a good chance that these people are also riddled with Adultitis, make terrible leaders, and will never change the world.

Consider the smartphone. It is a device on which you can look up any fact in the world or talk to your friend on the other side of the planet via video. And you can use it to order a hundred melon ballers that will arrive at your door by tomorrow. Just think of all the elements at play that make this thing work: microchips. The internet. Wi-Fi. Facial recognition. Speech recognition. Rechargeable battery. Unbreakable glass. (Oh, wait…)

Now, imagine having to explain all this stuff to your great-grandparents.

Preposterous!

For those of you old enough to remember TV shows from the twentieth century, it's something out of *The Jetsons* or *Star Trek*. But now it's just an ordinary, normal thing.

Okay, now let's compare this to a pocket calculator. The calculator seems simple by comparison, right?

What if I told you that the first handheld pocket calculator would not be invented until five years AFTER President John F. Kennedy declared, in 1961, that America would send a man to the moon by the end of the decade?

Preposterous!

Now let's look at some of the challenges you might be dealing with.

- Finding a better job.

- Paying off that credit card.

- Landing that account.

- Moving across the country.

- Completing that project on time.

- Finishing your degree.

- Potty-training your kid.

Do any of these issues seem all that hard by contrast?

Will success require creativity? Hard work? Sacrifice? Teamwork? Of course. But let's not label it as preposterous. It's amazing how many things that started out as preposterous eventually become rather obvious.

Remember, there once was a time when a stapler was a fancy piece of office equipment.

The Invasion of Nonsense

I love macarons. I had my first one only a few years ago, but it was love at first bite.

Not only am I always on the lookout for ways to get them into my belly, but I decided it was time to get them into some paintings. They're so cute and colorful, after all, and perhaps keeping myself busy painting them would distract me enough to keep me from eating them.

I like the whimsy that comes from playing with scale: making something smaller or bigger than it would be in real life. Perhaps this reflects my early fascination with dollhouses, dioramas, and *Micro Machine* cars.

One day, as I was doodling in my sketchbook, it occurred to me that a macaron looked a bit like a flying saucer. My imagination concocted a great scene in which an army of macaron UFOs descended upon a field of grazing cows. Naturally, one cow would have to be taken as a specimen for further experimentation, sucked up by a powerful tractor beam.

I like the idea that a painting like this begs the viewer to ponder some questions. What kind of planet did these strange, sweet ships come from? What will become of the cow? And where will the farmer imagine it went when he awakes in the morning to find one missing?

Yes, it's all nonsense. But that doesn't make it useless.

> **I like nonsense; it wakes up the brain cells.**
> –Dr. Seuss

Perhaps these nonsensical questions will wake up our brain cells so they will be firing on all cylinders when we need to tackle more vexing challenges in our lives. Answers tend to be found by people asking the most questions. And sometimes the answer to a problem is hiding in something that looks a lot like nonsense.

Maybe someday soon, one or more of Earth's most pressing problems will be solved, thanks to a discovery on some faraway planet. After all, it wasn't that long ago that space travel was nothing more than science fiction.

Sometimes nonsense makes the most sense of all.

"
some things have to be believed to be seen.

–Ralph Hodgson

"

the only prescription

Kotecki

More Cowbell Please

Somehow, the television show *Saturday Night Live* took a lowly old cowbell and turned it into a pop culture phenomenon. The famous skit imagines a studio session with the band Blue Oyster Cult recording their hit song "(Don't Fear) The Reaper." Christopher Walken, as "rock legend" Bruce Dickinson ("the cock of the walk, baby!"), singles out the little-used percussion instrument, played by Will Ferrell. Hilarity ensues as Dickinson urges the band to highlight the cowbell in the song.

Now the script was funny, and Walken and the other actors nailed their performances. But what is most interesting to me is that Ferrell and playwright Donnell Campbell, who co-wrote the sketch, first had to notice the cowbell in the original song by Blue Oyster Cult.

They noticed something most people didn't and saw an opportunity.

During a family vacation in Mexico, we bought a coconut drink from a roadside vendor for about $2. We enjoyed the drink and threw out the shell. (What else would we do with it?) Then I recalled some of the restaurants we visited where frozen drinks were served in coconut shells with tiny umbrellas. Undoubtedly, those drinks sold for a higher price than the same one served in a boring old glass. A "useless" coconut shell was transformed into something of value. Enterprising business owners had literally turned garbage into money.

Of course, flea markets and thrift stores do the exact same thing. And people who buy and flip fixer-uppers? Where most people see a dilapidated lost cause, they see a tidy profit and a future feature in a glossy magazine.

The most successful people see opportunities that others miss. I'd argue that it's not a talent; it's a habit.

In the middle of the Panic of 1873, a six-year recession, Thomas Edison invented the incandescent light bulb. In 1876, he established GE (General Electric Co.), which is now the third largest company in the world.

In the late 1970s, the United States experienced an energy crisis, and inflation ballooned out of control, causing a major recession which lasted for thirty months. In the midst of this economic storm, Applebee's, Ben & Jerry's, Olive Garden, and Fuddruckers were founded. In fact, all of the following entities were formed during a recession: Burger King, The Jim Henson Company, FedEx, CNN, Hewlett-Packard, MTV, Hyatt Hotels, Trader Joe's, *Sports Illustrated*, and Wikipedia.

The first Apple Store opened in the recession of 2001 and was declared dead on arrival. Which, of course, it wasn't; it was so successful that in the recession of 2008, many people considered Apple Stores to be recession-proof.

I remember talking to an elderly real estate tycoon during that economic nosedive of 2008. He grumbled about how all everyone seemed to do was complain about the bad economy. All he could see was an abundance of opportunities, and he lamented that he didn't have enough years left to take advantage of them all.

Most of the time, the difference between success and failure is determined by what we decide to see.

Indeed, the best time to buy stock is when the market is down. The best time to start a business is when the economy is bad. The best business ideas solve real problems.

We need you to look at the world as a child would, with big dreams, boundless optimism, and a vision of what's possible.

We need you to see through new eyes and find the opportunity that is right under your nose.

We need more cowbell.

96

"**every moment is a golden one** for him who has the **VISION** to recognize it as such."

–Henry Miller

The Good Old Days

A few years ago, I found myself lamenting the fact that our TV's remote control was on the fritz. It wasn't a battery issue; it was the power button that seemed to be on strike. I pegged my daughter Ginny (she was two at the time) as the prime suspect for its early demise. Although I had no hard evidence for that conclusion, she was often seen holding the remote, and the power button just so happened to be the only red button in a sea of black ones. I'm just saying.

Regardless of the culprit's identity, my frustration joined the chorus of a gazillion other parents who have crooned, "This is why we can't have nice things…"

On a seemingly unrelated note, one of the stops we made as a family during our western leg of the #Notarule Book Tour was De Smet, South Dakota. It's the location of one of Laura Ingalls Wilder's homesteads, and it offers a lot of interactive activities. Lucy had read all the books with her god-mom Jenna, and we'd been watching the television series together as a family. (They just don't make shows like that anymore, folks. And that Michael Landon was a real national treasure!) So of course we had to see this homestead.

One of the best parts of the trip was renting one of the four covered wagons available to sleep in overnight. It was also the worst night of sleep I've ever had. It's remarkable to think that our setup—we actually had electricity, so it wasn't exactly "roughing it"—would have been a dream to those early settlers.

Other discoveries were equally eye-opening. Covered wagons had wooden wheels—no shocks, struts, or satellite radio—and it took them all day to go fifteen miles. At one point, Laura and her family lived in a dugout, which was basically a dirt home carved out of a hillside; it had a single stove in the center and one window. Of course, there were no supermarkets around, so they had to provide their own food and make their own soap. One long winter, all they had to eat was plain old wheat bread, which had to be baked day after day, after grinding the flour by hand, and eaten without any butter. Also, and you can fact-check me on this, I don't think they had Amazon Prime.

My kids got to try washing and drying clothes the way people did laundry in the days before spin cycles and permanent press.

And the kids made corncob dolls just like the one Laura had. Honestly, I thought calling it a doll was a bit of a stretch. No face, no limbs, and certainly no karate-chop action.

It was a tremendous experience for all of us. I came away awed by the ingenuity of these pioneers amidst such humble circumstances, and grateful for the multitude of luxuries I take for granted in my own life.

It's amazing how a change in perspective really can change everything.

Which is to say, after that trip, I was magically no longer all that concerned with the malfunctioning power button on my remote control.

Consider this: The average income, around the world, is five thousand dollars. If you make more than that, then you're in the top 50 percent. If you make more than fifty thousand dollars, you're in the top 0.5 percent.

We live in a time when Oregon Trail is a fun computer game, not a harrowing months-long journey replete with danger and dysentery.

Are you alive? Do you have a job? Do you have a roof over your head? Do you have something to eat today? Does someone love you? Do you have a dream in your heart? Is today a chance to let go of yesterday and start fresh? Although you may not have said yes to every single one of those questions, I'm betting you can say yes to most.

And if that's true, regardless of what goals remain unattained or what inconveniences are currently plaguing us, I think we can agree that our lives are pretty dang good.

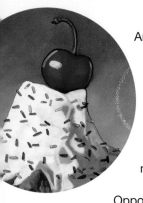

Anything else is a cherry on top.

We all have challenges. Some are crazy big ones. Others, like my temperamental remote control, are molehills disguised as mountains. In either case, dwelling on them endlessly only drives us to a deep sense of fearful paralysis. And while we are tirelessly focusing on how bad things are, what are we missing out on?

Opportunities, for one. And reasons to be grateful.

There's a popular phrase people use when reflecting on their pasts: "Those were the good old days." Ever notice how nobody ever says, ***"These** are the good old days"*?

Hmm. What if you—right now—were currently smack-dab in the middle of your good old days?

Think about it. Before you—right now—are opportunities, moments, and blessings you'll never experience again. You have people in your life right now that you won't have with you forever. Maybe not next year. Are you appreciating them? Or are you taking the good things for granted while you focus on your fears?

Ever find yourself saying, "Life will be better when …"?

If you're a parent, you can fill in the blank mighty easily. Life will be better when …

… he can sleep through the night.

… she can feed herself.

… he can tell us where it hurts.

… she goes to school.

… he makes it to the NBA and buys me a ginormous house in Hawaii.

This is a diabolical game that Adultitis likes us to play, because it gets us wishing away time, distracts us from the present, and keeps us focused on the negative.

Of course, this pastime is not exclusive to parenthood. We can do it our whole lives if we're not careful. As in, "Life will be easier when I graduate, when I get that promotion, when I move to that new apartment, when we get married, when we have kids, when the kids move out, when I finally retire," and on and on.

Then one day you wake up, wondering where the time went and yearning for the "good old days."

No doubt about it, certain aspects of life DO get easier as we move from stage to stage. What's easy to forget is that a whole new crop of challenges and problems comes with each next stage. The reality is this: no matter what stage of life you find yourself in, there are pleasant things and not-so-pleasant things about it. No exceptions.

The only people without challenges are taking up residence in the extended-stay resorts called cemeteries.

My dad told me that he and Mom used to look forward to the day when we kids were out on our own. "I assumed that we wouldn't have to worry so much about you guys," he said. "But then you all got married, and our family—and the number of people to worry about—tripled. Now we have grandkids to worry about, too!"

Even though my brothers and I are self-sufficient and successful, we've all encountered various storms that come with life. Challenges that make diaper changing and carpooling seem like a walk in the park. Or as our mom puts it: "When you have little people, you have little problems. Big people have bigger problems."

Instead of focusing on the negatives and waiting for circumstances to get easier, you can focus on the positive and appreciate the good things about your current situation. The stuff you'll miss. There's *always* something.

For instance, life IS easier now that my kids can entertain themselves for more than seven seconds, but I already miss sleeping on the couch holding my bundles of joy. Likewise, before we bought our first home, there wasn't much I liked about our old apartment. But living in Wisconsin, I always tried to appreciate that I wasn't the one responsible for shoveling the snow.

If you find Adultitis urging you to pine for a time when life will get easier, use it as an opportunity to instead focus on something good about your current season of life.

Relish the fact that you, right now, are living in the good old days.

At the very least, be grateful that you don't have to make your own shampoo.

half FULL

Kotecki

Half Full

I like to think of myself as an optimistic person. After all, I am a lifelong Cubs fan who has always believed in the hope-filled power of next year. Then again, when they lose three games in a row these days, my certainty that they'll never win another game makes me feel like a pessimist.

The truth is, I'm probably a little bit of both.

The optimistic side of me believed that *Penguins Can't Fly* would be a New York Times bestseller. It wasn't. (At least not yet.)

This defeat, along with a number of other failures in my career, add up to bolster the popular argument that I should minimize the chances of pain and defeat by keeping my expectations low.

This strategy of operating with low expectations is employed by many. The thinking goes that if you don't get your hopes up about something, then you won't be as disappointed if it doesn't work out. And if it turns out well, you'll get the enjoyment of being pleasantly surprised.

This strategy is flawed for several reasons.

According to neuroscientist Tali Sharot, author of *The Science of Optimism*, people with high expectations always feel better about themselves because how we feel depends on how we interpret events. When a person with high expectations succeeds, they attribute it to their own traits. When they fail, it wasn't because they were dumb; it was because the exam happened to be unfair, and next time they'll do better. When a person with low expectations fails, it was because they were dumb, and if they succeed, it's because the exam happened to be easy, and next time, reality will catch up with them.

Furthermore, regardless of the outcome, the act of anticipation makes us happy. It's why people prefer Friday to Sunday: Friday brings with it the anticipation of the weekend ahead.

Finally, optimism acts as a self-fulfilling prophecy. Believing we will be successful makes us more likely to be so, and optimism reduces stress and anxiety, leading to better health.

When a container is at 50 percent capacity, it is half full. Technically, it's also half empty.

Both descriptions are absolutely correct assessments of the container in question.

If the label you give an event is completely subjective, go with the label that gives you the best chance of going somewhere beyond what you thought was possible.

So many of our experiences in life could be seen in the same light. We lose a job. We break a leg. We get dumped by the one we thought was The One. Is that unexpected, unwelcome thing that just happened in your life an obstacle or an opportunity?

Yes.

Both are absolutely correct assessments of the event in question.

Deciding what you call it can make all the difference.

Was *Penguins Can't Fly* a failure?

Upon further review, our team's belief that the book could be a bestseller led us to put in a lot of effort. It pushed us to think of new and creative ways to promote it, and it got me out of my comfort zone in asking for help. All of these initiatives made a difference. No, it wasn't a NYT bestseller, but three printings later, it was a success. The book sold well enough for me to earn back my advance (something most published authors never do) and more.

I believe that my optimism contributed to that success. Without the optimism and accompanying efforts, I would always have wondered what might have been.

I don't know if I'm naturally optimistic or not. These days, even though I still feel fearful about getting my hopes up only to have them dashed, I'm realizing that optimism is more of a choice than a disposition.

We all get to make that choice every single day. To me, there's no contest.

I choose half full.

"we can complain because rose bushes have **thorns** or rejoice that thorn bushes have **roses.**

–Anonymous

"

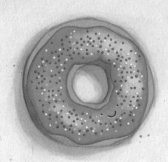

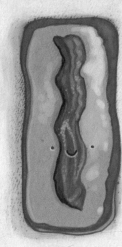

LifE
is
SwEEt

Kotecki

Doughnuts and Optimism

I love painting doughnuts. They are sweet and whimsical and evoke feelings of nostalgia, which is how some people might describe my artwork. I'd probably be content to paint nothing more than doughnuts for the rest of my life.

Only one problem.

Every time I paint doughnuts, I want to eat them. Which is not sustainable, unless I add "getting cut out of my home and removed via crane" to my bucket list, which I'd rather not.

You know what is sustainable? Optimism. Deciding to look on the bright side and find the good in every person and every situation. It sustains us in the good times and the bad times, with no discernible downsides.

Sadly, people who are regularly optimistic are often viewed in the same light as doughnuts: nice and sweet, but completely lacking in any nutritional substance.

To the cynics of the world, an optimistic person is an intellectual lightweight. A simpleton. Blind to the realities of the world.

I submit that the way of the cynic is the easy way. Although smugly disguised in trendy hipster jeans and an ironic smile, cynicism is the lazy way out. It takes no special skill to identify negatives, assume the worst, and rain down judgment on everyone else.

Check your social media feed to see if I'm right.

In our self-help culture, we have thousands of books at our disposal that will tell us how to be happy. We keep buying them, hoping that the sheer act of reading them will transform us, as if there is some secret bit of knowledge that has not yet been revealed to mankind—or at least to us—that will change everything. But the advice is always the same, so we skip it, concluding that it didn't work.

Reading about something is not the same as doing it. The doing part is always harder than the reading part.

Although I know naturally optimistic people, optimism remains a choice. You can choose to see the good in every person and every situation, no matter how dire or despicable.

Now, is it easy? Hells, no.

Being kind and respectful to a person who has opposing political views? Hard.

Looking for the good when your family has been blindsided by a devastating illness? Hard.

Straining to see something redeemable in that jerk at work? Hard.

Finding reasons to be grateful when you're out of work and have no money to buy Christmas gifts for your kids? Hard.

Of course, we'd rather have our situation change. We'd rather have the other guy change. We'd rather have that policy change. But if we have the courage to change ourselves, everything changes.

Living a life filled with peace, joy, and happiness is no easy task. There is no magic pill. It can't be delivered via FedEx. But being cynical isn't the answer; it's just a one-way ticket in the wrong direction.

Optimism has no downside.

Heck, the best way to turn any bad mood into a good one is to change your perspective from cynical to optimistic and begin counting all the blessings you are thankful for.

Starting with doughnuts.

organic
I wish i was JUICIER.
i wish i was CRUNCHIER.
must be nice
Kotecki

Must Be Nice

It's a natural human tendency to compare ourselves to others, especially to people who are in the same field we're in. Comparison isn't necessarily a bad thing if it leads us to discover areas where we can improve. But when it shifts into envy or jealousy, that's a problem.

I often attend the annual convention for the National Speakers Association. I always have to brace myself for the "must be nice" game. In the speaker world, it goes like this:

Of course he gets booked all the time, he's a former NBA player. Must be nice.

She's got so many connections from working all those years in the corporate world. Must be nice.

I wish I could juggle fire and do backflips like that. Must be nice.

I spend so much time noticing all the things I'm not that I miss the things I am.

One theme that drove itself home for me during a convention years ago was my talent as an artist. It's something I'm good at, and it's a skill that very few speakers possess. And yet incorporating my artistic gifts into my speaking programs and offerings was almost an afterthought. I had not yet made it a cornerstone of who I am and what I do.

This small revelation of mine might be patently obvious to you, as it is to many speaker friends I've shared it with. Interestingly, our greatest gifts are often the ones we overlook the most because we tend to undervalue the abilities that come easily to us.

At some point, I realized that were I to devote the time and attention to making my art an integral part of my unique selling proposition, there would inevitably be those who'd observe me from afar and say, "Of course he's a successful speaker. Being a great artist is a killer hook and he can make his PowerPoint slides look amazing. Must be nice."

Since that fateful convention, I have made art the foundation of my offerings. And people do in fact think it must be nice.

Meanwhile, I have a wife who shares my passion for fighting Adultitis and who is very good at communicating with clients and managing travel details. She books all my gigs and handles all my travel arrangements. Must be nice, huh?

You're dang right it is!

Now, the "must be nice" game is not exclusive to the speaking world. In your world, it might look like this:

Of course she is the top performer; she has a ton of contacts. Must be nice.

Everybody likes him because he is a natural-born comedian. Must be nice.

She's tall and athletic and got a free ride to college because she's a great volleyball player. Must be nice.

He is able to afford a house like that because he's a carpenter and can do all the labor himself. Must be nice.

Of course they get to travel all the time; they don't have any kids. Must be nice.

He gets straight A's and he doesn't even have to study. Must be nice.

She has all the time in the world to be involved in her kids' activities; her husband has a great job and she doesn't have to work. Must be nice.

The "must be nice" we tack on at the end is our backhanded way of voicing our envy and making excuses for ourselves. It's also a cop-out and a tragic waste of time. First of all, when all you see is the highlight reel, you miss the shortcomings that drive people crazy and the hard battles they are fighting quietly. Like my dad says, "The grass may look greener on the other side, but it still has to be cut."

Our propensity to succumb to jealousy in this way is a distraction from a most important truth: **We all have a "must be nice."**

Everyone has unique gifts and circumstances and experiences that they can leverage and benefit from. Including you.

Your job is to quit wishing for someone else's, figure out what yours is, and make the most of it.

What's your "must be nice?"

"to see what is in front of one's nose needs a constant struggle.

–George Orwell

How to Be Lucky

Lucky is winning a game of Candy Land against my daughter.

Many things in life that seem lucky are often anything but. Oftentimes it's merely the result of a lot of hard work.

Undoubtedly, where you are born, who your parents are, the color of your skin, and whether or not you grow up to be 6-foot-8 with the ability to jump over a school bus are completely out of your control and could all be considered "luck." And yet, having any of these so-called advantages is no guarantee of success, while not having them does not condemn you to certain failure. Every NBA draft class is filled with dudes who won the genetic lottery but don't last long in the league.

I could be all bent out of shape because my gifts are not advantageous to playing professional basketball. But we are all given different gifts that become our advantages. True joy and fulfillment are the result of fashioning a life that utilizes those gifts to the best of our abilities in the service of others.

> **"Luck is what happens when preparation meets opportunity."** –Seneca, Roman philosopher

Luck is out of your control. But you know what isn't? Finding the courage, discipline, and persistence to try something that might not work. See also: putting in the hours, perfecting your craft, and getting back up after you fail. Sometimes the hardest work is keeping your faith when everyone else paints you a fool.

You have the good fortune to be alive, right now, with an abundance of realized and untapped gifts and talents. What you do with them next has nothing to do with luck.

Want some good fortune? **Be good at what you do, and be a good person.**

Spend your life working on those two things, and the luck part often has a way of taking care of itself.

The Night Light

When you were a child, were you ever afraid of the dark? I sure was. From horns and hair to scabs and skeletons, thinking about what lurked among the shadows was an all-you-can-eat buffet for my imagination.

I might not have made it through childhood without that humble but powerful life-saving device known as the nightlight. Although small in size and wattage, it did a remarkable job of keeping the creepy-crawlies at bay. Without it, I'm sure I'd have been digested in the belly of a slimy beast from the netherworld known as Underthebed.

Many lives have been saved by the simple nightlight. Perhaps it wouldn't have been needed if we'd only believed our parents when they told us that there aren't any monsters under the bed; they're only in our imaginations.

But alas, parents are never very convincing.

Perhaps that is because grownups also deal with monsters. They just live in a different place. You see, as we get older, the monsters move out from under our beds and move up, into our heads.

Think I'm nuts?

How many times have you lain awake at night, worried, scared, or anxious about any number of things? These fears keep us up, and they can wreak some terrifying results.

Our parents were on to something when they tucked us into bed and tried to calm our fears about the monsters. You know, the part where they told us that the monsters exist only in our imaginations.

That's the key word to keep in mind: imagination.

Think back to when you were five years old. Maybe you had a window in your bedroom. And maybe just outside that window was a tree. By day, that tree looked like an ordinary tree. Harmless. Almost friendly, even.

But at night, that tree cast some weird shadows into your room. Right before your eyes, it somehow transformed into an enormous, ravenous T-Rex, with dagger teeth and jagged claws, ever reaching in your direction. Ominously, it eyed you, tucked into your sheets and blankets and looking a lot like a ravioli-shaped midnight snack.

Looking back with the advantage of years and wisdom, you know there was no T-Rex lurking outside your bedroom window. It was just that tree, casting shadows that made your imagination run wild, concocting spine-chilling possibilities that you couldn't help but believe.

Our imaginations are quite good at what they do.

Here's the thing: No matter how creative we think we are (or aren't), our imaginations don't shut off just because we're adults now. The stuff that keeps us up at night now is still largely the product of an overactive imagination.

That's not true, I hear you saying. *The stuff I'm worried about is real-world stuff. Things like my job and my mortgage and my kids.*

Okay, I hear you. But now hear this: Most of the stuff we worry about never happens.

I'll say it again: Most of the stuff we worry about never happens.

Think back over the last year and call to mind all of the things you spent time worrying about. I'll bet you that most of that stuff didn't amount to anything at all. And the less-than-ideal instances that did come to pass were nowhere near as frightening as your imagination led you to believe.

Just as they did with the ominous shadows slithering across our bedroom floors, our imaginations take kernels of doubt and the vast unknown and concoct possible future outcomes. Outcomes that more times than not give us the heebie-jeebies.

It is an interesting trait of human nature that when it comes to imagination and our future, we automatically move more toward the negative than the positive. Think about it. You hear rumors about possible layoffs at work. Do you naturally assume that your job will be unaffected and begin expecting a promotion? Or does your train of thought lead to a scenario that has you being the first one cut, resulting in your being unable to pay your mortgage, having your house foreclosed on, and living under a bridge eating Spam out of a can?

The negative outcomes tend to be the ones our imaginations spend the most time on and the ones that keep us up at night. So, what's a person supposed to do about this?

Here's what I am proposing: First, let us acknowledge that the stuff that contributes to our uncertainty and anxiousness is largely attributable to our imaginations. Once we can accept that, let's put our imaginations to work for us, instead of against us.

If you are wracked with fear over a particular issue, be it large or small, begin by letting your imagination do what it wants to do anyway: go negative. That's right; pull out a sheet of paper and write down the absolute **worst** possible outcome you can imagine. This should come quite easily, as it is the thing that's been stealing your peace of mind for so long. Don't leave out any gory details, including instantaneous death by embarrassment or a new career as a bum or a bag lady.

Now, once you are scared senseless and ready to pee your pants, take out another sheet of paper and write down the **best** possible outcome you can dream up. It may take a while for your imagination to kick into high gear, but when it does, reach for the sky. We're talking fantasy land, pie-in-the-sky, Hollywood-couldn't-write-it-because-it's-too-unbelievable type of craziness. Have fun with it.

Okay, now that you've balanced things out a bit, take out a third (and final) sheet of paper and write down what you imagine to be the **likely** outcome of your particular scenario. This will probably fall somewhere in between the first two outcomes. It might be a bit uncomfortable or unpleasant, but it will be nowhere near as terrifying as you first suspected.

This activity is a simple one, but if you give it a shot, it won't be long before a sense of peace starts to descend upon you. Writing out the scary stuff that's in your head is like shining a light on the situation. It clarifies the facts—that tree really is just a tree—and helps us to see just how ridiculous our initial assessment of the situation was.

A T-Rex?! Phfffft. Those went extinct a million years ago!

The monsters that terrorized you years ago have much in common with the ones that kept you up last night. Imagination is a powerful tool, and with some guidance, it can serve as a helpful nightlight that guides us to a peaceful present and a future that is better than we ever expected.

Sweet dreams!

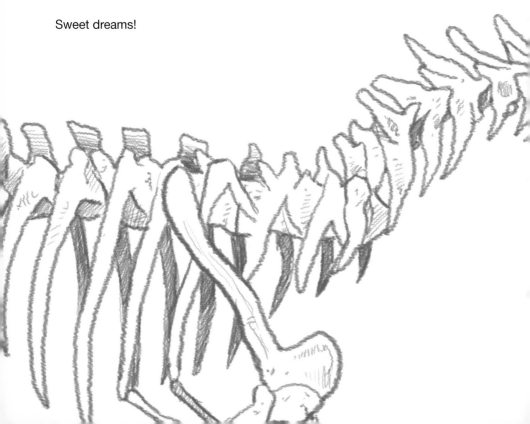

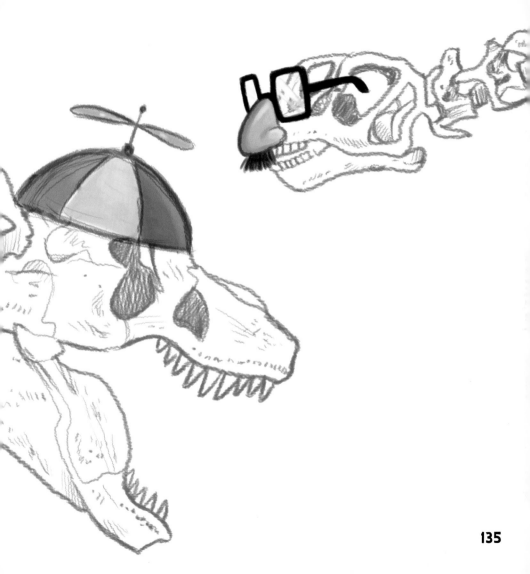

ROCKET

yeah

What If It Works?

We've been launching ourselves into space for decades now, and there's still an element of risk every time we do it. Although very smart people do their best to minimize it, there is always the prospect of danger and disaster. With all that humankind has gained from these amazing missions, I'm thankful that we've had so many brave people willing to go for the ride.

It's good to remember that every worthwhile endeavor comes with an element of risk and requires at least some small measure of bravery. It comes with the territory and is a necessary consideration as we make our plans.

However, I made this painting to also remind us not to focus too much on the danger.

I know I can get sucked into spending too much time thinking about the risks— about what I might lose and what people will think of me if I fail (especially if I fail in some spectacular fashion).

Determining that an endeavor carries some risk shouldn't automatically keep us from moving forward.

The whimsy incorporated into this piece, in the form of a bomb pop blasting off into space, is a reminder to focus on the excitement of what's possible and the potential gains to be made in the process of trying. This recalibration can give us the fuel we need to launch ourselves into an adventure in which the outcome is unknown.

Do you have an opportunity in front of you that's freaking you out a little bit?

Instead of worrying so much about what might happen if it doesn't work, get excited by asking yourself the question,

"What if it does?!"

"if your vision doesn't scare you, then both your vision and your god are too small.

—Brother Andrew

Not Sunk Yet

Many people come up to me after my speaking programs and say, "I wish I would've heard you when my kids were young." There is sadness and regret over what are perceived as missed opportunities.

I get it. One of the reasons I do what I do is to make sure people have as few "if onlys" as possible. But you can't sail toward the bright future in front of you when you're anchored to the "if onlys" of the past.

I've seen movies that start slowly, barely holding my attention. There's not a lot going on. It's unremarkable. But sometimes there is a spark, a turning point that catapults the story into a thrilling new direction. Suddenly I'm completely engaged, drawn into the story and excited to see how it ends.

Life can be like that. We get caught up in the river of rules and expectations set forth by others, and the current pulls us in a predictable direction. It's safe and plain and comfortable, with nothing too exciting going on.

But sometimes there is a spark, a moment that jolts us into a new way of thinking and an opportunity for a fresh start.

We all have backstories—dark times, skeletons in our closets, or even just the regretful ache of time wasted. If we could go back in time, I'm sure everyone would have at least one thing they'd like to do differently. But until we can figure out how to bend time with DeLoreans going eighty-eight miles per hour, that is a pipe dream. Feel sad, sure, but use that sadness to fuel a change. See that spark as the gift that it is: an opportunity—and an obligation!—to do better right now.

Despite the missteps or missed opportunities you've experienced, know this: the credits have not yet rolled. You are not finished.

You can't change the beginning of your story, but you can change the ending.

If you are still breathing, there is still story to be told.

"

it's not foresight or hindsight we need. we need sight, plain and simple. we need to see what is right in front of us.

–Gordon Atkinson

"

ready for lift off

Ready for Lift-Off

One time, Kim and I spent a couple hundred dollars on a booth at a two-day craft show. That was a big chunk of change for us at the time—about two months' worth of groceries. We were next to a booth where a guy was selling knockoff Garfield tchotchkes. Meanwhile, we moved a grand total of $7.94 worth of greeting cards. It was rough. Then we drowned our sorrows in sirloin steaks at Outback, which made our negative profit margin even worse.

I have a lot of stories like that from the early days. Happy times.

I have often felt like this hippo: barely off the ground, just trying to get some lift, with very little progress to show for a heck of a lot of effort.

But then I think of situations like that craft show, and I'm impressed and a little surprised by how far we've come. We feel a great sense of satisfaction in what we've built and accomplished, regardless of how much distance there is left to cover.

More time than you think it should.

Like way more.

We need to hear that reminder often because it applies to everything from dream businesses and amazing relationships to paying off Bank of America and mastering the clarinet. Progress always seems to be taking longer than it should, thanks to microwave ovens and Usain Bolt, to name a few reasons. The media peddle their stories of overnight success. *These people catapulted to fame and fortune in one fell swoop; why can't you?*

If there were get-rich-quick schemes that actually worked, I'd be writing this on my yacht and you'd be reading it on yours.

Back in the early days, when progress was slower than a sloth on Ambien and failures mounted like a population of mogwai at a waterpark, one thing helped me persevere: the thought that *this* could be the day that changes everything. This could be the idea that catches fire. This could be the day that one of my creations goes viral. This could be the day that Oprah calls and we hug and cry and laugh together.

Even though I have yet to have "that day," that hope has kept me going, day by day, and in the meantime, the days and weeks and years have piled up and turned into something real that supports my family, helps make the world a little better, and makes me feel proud.

Are you trying to accomplish something great? Please, stick with it. Yes, keep working on improving yourself. Tinker, and do more of what works. But don't be discouraged by your seeming lack of progress.

It can take a long time for something big to get off the ground, but once it does, it's a sight to behold.

Keep On Fishing

You can spend all day fishing and catch nothing: 2,375 casts; 2,375 failures.

But.

The next cast could be the one that changes everything.

Since I started my company in 1999, I've encountered many dead ends. We've had a lot of projects we were excited about, initiatives we were certain would deliver the breakthrough beyond our wildest dreams, that failed—hard.

We've lost money, time, and pride. Sometimes, it's taken a long time to recover. After you've been hit by a car so many times, you start to wonder if maybe you should stop standing in the middle of the highway.

But one thing that kept me going was a quote by Thomas Edison, who said, "Many of life's failures are people who did not realize how close they were to success when they gave up."

I guess I was more afraid of being a failure than I was of failing. And there's a difference.

Dead ends happen. But hitting one doesn't necessarily mean you're dead or at the end.

The hope that the big breakthrough could be just around the corner was the fuel I needed to pick myself up from my failures and keep going. Maybe that's all God needed from me at those times when I was working on enterprises that would never pan out: to just keep going. He was working behind the scenes, on me and on the other things and people that just needed time.

Interestingly, I'm still waiting for that big breakthrough. But the process of getting back up and trying something a little different after each failure has bought me enough time for small breakthroughs to pile up. And those little breakthroughs have added up to something pretty special.

No, if something's not working, you shouldn't keep doing the same thing over and over again. Try a new type of bait. Change your technique. Move to a new location.

But keep casting.

> "every great work, every great accomplishment, has been brought into manifestation through holding to the vision, and often just before the big achievement, comes apparent failure and discouragement.

–Florence Scovel Shinn

Pie in the Sky

In December 2016, I wrote the biggest check of my life. Not in size, but in importance. It was the final check to close out a business debt that totaled $100,000 back in 2008. We paid it off seven months early, and for the first time since we launched in 2000, the business was completely debt-free.

That felt really good.

Deep down, I always knew we'd pay it off, but it felt like it would take forever. In 2008, the year 2017 seemed a million years away. And before that, as we racked up said debt to stay afloat while we tested business models and funded small successes (and a few big defeats), surviving—let alone thriving—seemed impossible.

At least it did when we spent two whole days at a craft show in Milwaukee and sold only $7.94 worth of greeting cards.

Or when my hometown newspaper, which ran my comic strip free for a whole year, decided to drop it when I asked for $10 a week.

Or when we were down to the last $100 in our bank account more times than I care to remember.

Pie in the sky.

Coined in a song written in 1911 by a Swedish-born American named Joe Hill, the phrase "pie in the sky" represents an idea that is good and pleasant to contemplate, but very unlikely to be realized.

I don't know what the odds were of our building a successful business with no experience, no proven business model, and no money. Were they as big as the Cubs rallying from a 3–1 series deficit to win the World Series? Or as unlikely as the Patriots coming back from 25 down, with just over a quarter left to play, to win the Super Bowl?

The real question is this: How great does the deck have to be stacked against you before you give up, labeling your dream as pie in the sky?

Only you have an answer for that, and every person has a different one. But we are often too quick to chalk something up as pie in the sky when it really isn't. That premature assessment can keep us from even starting. It lets us off the hook, thinking our dream was impossible anyway, because sacrifice and hard work and hope—yes, even hope—hurt sometimes.

I don't write this to place myself on a pedestal. If I have done anything well, it has been to persist. My persistence was fueled by a belief that God had placed this dream deep in my heart and that He would see it through. Every day I woke up thinking, *This could be the day*—the day that we got our big break and everything would turn around. Some of the opportunities that looked like big breaks turned out to be pathetic spurts and epic fails. Mostly we got a lot of small breaks that added up to something great. The long process certainly tested every bit of my patience and nerve and good sense and made me question my sanity on more than thirty-seven occasions, but here we are.

Not every endeavor is worth seeing through 'till the end. As we grow, our dreams and desires and priorities can change. Don't be tricked into stopping just because the odds seem long, though. Everything is impossible until it isn't.

Yes, the odds may be long. Your stamina may be depleted. Your hope may be dim.

But if the cause is great enough and your soul is on board and your motive is pure, keep going.

You may just be able to grab that pie and eat it, too.

Wind in Our Sails

This painting was inspired by a family vacation in Mexico. One thing that stood out was the abundance of color I saw in the clothing, architecture, and artwork. When you're accustomed to everything being Pottery Barn beige and gray, all that color really stands out.

I wanted to incorporate that vibrant, whimsical color, along with one of the culture's great traditions, *Dia de Muertos*, or Day of the Dead, into a painting. I think that tradition is a beautiful way to look at the afterlife and our ancestors. I appreciated the idea of seeing death as a part of the process of life, rather than as just an ending.

I also liked the focus on how much we owe to the people who came before us. American culture celebrates the independent spirit of the individual. That's fine, as far as it goes. Except that there is no such thing as a self-made man or woman. No one becomes successful by themselves. Yes, your unique talents and a fiery self-determination are key ingredients for success, but life is a group effort.

I was thinking about the people in my own life who have passed away. Not just family members, but also teachers and coaches who served as mentors. Every one of them taught me something that I carry with me to this day.

My Grandma K. made me feel like I was special, just as I was.

My third-grade teacher, Mrs. Smith, encouraged me to take my artistic talent seriously.

My Little League coach, Mr. Dawson, helped me believe that I was a winner.

When I was an uncertain teenager, Deacon Vince saw me as a grown-up with valuable contributions to make.

Each of us is like that tiny sailboat in my painting. At times, it can feel like we are drifting, alone, on a vast and overwhelming sea.

But we are not alone.

We have the wisdom given to us by the people who have gone before us. Their examples live on, showing us the way, and their words live on as the wind in our sails, guiding us into a bright and colorful future.

"if i have seen
further than others,
it is by standing
upon the shoulders
of giants.

–Isaac Newton

cupcakes are muffins that believed in miracles

Look for Miracles

In third grade, my teacher, Mrs. Smith, asked me to draw Santa for the school newsletter because she said I could draw him better than she could. That floored me and gave me a lot of confidence. She had noticed something good and told me about it.

And so I kept drawing. I loved the escape it created. Hours would pass in an instant.

I noticed that if I made my pictures look like who or what they were supposed to look like, people seemed to like that.

So, I made copies. Really good copies. I drew Simpsons characters and portraits of athletes. That was okay for a while; it was how I learned my craft. As author Elizabeth Gilbert reminds us, "Everybody imitates before they can innovate."

I liked drawing people because I liked how people reacted when I captured a likeness accurately.

As I got older, I became intrigued by the idea of not just copying a photograph, but making creative choices that helped accentuate something about that person's personality or character.

My first real attempt at saying something original was through comics—first a sports panel cartoon called *Obstructed View*, then a strip called *Kim & Jason*. I became inspired by artists like Charles Schulz (*Peanuts*) and Sam Butcher (*Precious Moments*), and I decided that I wanted to use my art to make a difference. I was convinced that *Kim & Jason* was the way I was destined to do that. I had big dreams, and Kim and I worked hard to get the word out about my comic strip and characters.

I was undeterred by the scores of syndicate rejections. We tried self-syndication. Craft fairs. Gift shows. Fundraising programs. Some initiatives were moderately successful. Most failed epically. None of them earned enough for us to live on, and Kim and I had many sleepless nights and tear-filled discussions, wondering if we were crazy.

My experience creating a comic strip led to presenting cartooning workshops in schools, which led to speaking at churches, which led to speaking for associations and companies. Speaking became more financially successful than

Kim & Jason ever was, and eventually, I became so busy that after seven years of making a daily comic, I decided to retire the strip for good.

Although *Kim & Jason* inspired many people with smiles and laughter, it was hard not to think of my art as a total failure. As my speaking career took off, I put the "art thing" in the closet. I figured that my attempt to be an artist had failed and decided to focus on more "valuable" projects. And so even though I got to use my creativity in many ways while growing the business, I pretty much stopped making art.

After several years of inactivity—I now self-importantly call it my fallow period—I started to feel the urge to make art again. I began to feel alive in a way I hadn't felt in a long time. And I started to realize that after all these years, I finally had something to say.

So, I kept making this new art. I shared it. And people responded, not just to how it was made but also to how it made them feel. And think.

I got my first book deal with a huge New York publisher largely because a literary agent saw some art that was shared by a friend of a friend on Facebook. While designing *Penguins Can't Fly*, I marveled at the fact that 90 percent of the art in it was created after my fallow period. But the book also contained stories, comic strips, and paintings from years earlier. It became a love letter to the efforts in my past that I thought were failures.

I finally realized that they weren't failures; they were the foundation of my current business.

In 2017, we hosted the first-ever Wondernite, a special art-collecting event that featured my newest works, all of which were created in the previous two years. Ten years earlier, when I made the tough decision to retire *Kim & Jason*, if you'd have told me that new art I'd create would help me land a book deal, and that we'd be able to pull off an event like Wondernite, fill it to capacity, and make thousands of dollars selling the majority of the original art I'd brought, I wouldn't have believed you. I might have punched you in the face for being mean.

To me, how this journey ultimately unfolded feels very much like a miracle.

Miracles happen. I've seen them, in my own life and in the lives of others. Frustratingly, they are unpredictable and cannot be conjured up on demand.

I have had my heart broken many times by dreams that didn't come true and miracles that never materialized. I have been tempted to give up on them, to quit dreaming and stop waiting for miracles. It seems easier. Less painful. You know, expect the worst and be surprised when something good happens.

But I just can't give up.

I don't know why sometimes a miracle shows up while other times it doesn't. Maybe it's because what we get instead is even better in the long run. Maybe it's just random luck or something else entirely.

Whatever it is, I can't shake the belief that it's still worth believing in them.

It seems like the people who see miracles are the ones who spend more time looking for them.

happy girls are *Prettiest*

kotecki

What Is Beautiful?

You can't write a book about seeing without talking about beauty.

It has been said that beauty is in the eye of the beholder. But what if the beholder changes his or her mind?

Art history class is where I first learned that the ideal of beauty has changed a lot over the centuries. The sculptures of round, full-figured fertility goddesses from primitive cultures looked nothing like the airbrushed models I saw in the *Sports Illustrated* swimsuit issue each year. I later realized that even Marilyn Monroe, the sex icon of the 1950s, might be labeled as "fat" by today's standards.

As the father of two daughters, I don't want their definition of beauty to be determined by people trying to sell glossy magazines or goopy cream in bottles.

So, if what we consider beautiful changes over time, we can decide to change our definition of beauty now.

Sometimes my wife complains about her crow's feet, but when I look into her eyes, they are happy. And to me, that is incredibly sexy.

You can have your lipsticks, your lotions, and your pouty pursed lips. To me, happy girls are prettiest.

My daughter Ginny loves to dress up in fancy dresses. She is beautiful. But you know when she is most beautiful? When she is laughing and giggling, caught up in a simple moment and filled with joy. There is nothing, and I mean nothing, more beautiful than that.

There is something magically irresistible about people who are happy. We are drawn to them. We want to be around them. We want to bask in their happiness.

So, allow me to write a little something to my daughters:

How exactly do you become happy? Well, beating yourself up because your this *is too big and your* that *is too small is a rather poor strategy.*

A quote often attributed to Abraham Lincoln states, "People are just about as happy as they make up their minds to be." It would appear that the first step toward happiness is to decide to be happy.

You can feel justified in this decision because you were made by a loving God, the same one who invented rainbows and sunsets and the sounds that

birds make in the springtime. You, with your quirks and your imperfections, make Him smile with pride.

So dance and sing and laugh and love. Chase your bliss instead of the approval of people who don't matter. Embrace the things that light you up, not the things that only seem to bring you down. Delight in the little joys, and laugh at the things that you find funny. Own your guilty pleasures, not the guilt of thinking you're not good enough.

Don't try to make yourself beautiful in order to be happy.

Be happy because you are already beautiful.

How Many Licks?

How many licks does it take to get to the Tootsie Roll center of a Tootsie Pop?

A commercial that appeared on TV when I was a child asked that very question. Well, a number of folks have tried to solve this mystery.

A group of engineering students from Purdue University built a licking machine, modeled after a human tongue, and determined that it took an average of 364 licks to get to the center of a Tootsie Pop. A chemical engineering student from the University of Michigan built his own licking machine and recorded that his required 411 licks. And a group of junior high school students ditched machines in favor of human lickers and reported an average of 144 licks.

Apparently, the world may never know how many licks it takes to get to the Tootsie Roll center of a Tootsie Pop.

We humans love to measure things. It brings a sense of certainty to a life that's not all that certain.

A few years ago, Kim and I went to the funeral of a friend's mom. She had died suddenly of a heart attack while at home with her husband, who was in only his second week of retirement. When my father-in-law, Gary, heard the news and learned that they were both in the same age range, he reflected, "Wow. I guess I'm really on borrowed time."

He's right. But not just because he was diagnosed with severe rheumatoid arthritis in his twenties and probably hasn't had a pain-free day since then. And not just because he continues to amaze his doctors with how long he's been able to keep going. He's right because we are ALL on borrowed time.

That becomes obvious when we hear of heart attacks and car accidents, when we are faced with stories of tornadoes dropping out of the sky, ending lives at random, or when we see the devastating aftermath of troubled souls deciding that children are suitable targets for acts of terrorism.

Life expectancy may be seventy-eight, but that doesn't mean we can expect to make it there.

Gary is on borrowed time. I'm on borrowed time. And so are you. The real question is, how are we investing this time we are borrowing?

By watching more TV? Keeping busy with activities that don't really matter? Staying put on a career path we don't really like?

Or are we building something wonderful by living with a sense of urgency and making hard choices that lead to a better story and a lasting legacy?

In 2007, comedian Bernie Mac told David Letterman on CBS's *Late Show* that he planned to retire soon. "I'm going to still do my producing, my films, but I want to enjoy my life a little bit," he said. "I missed a lot of things, you know. I was a street performer for two years. I went into clubs in 1977."

I don't know what Bernie meant by "soon" in regards to his retirement, but sadly, he was dead a year later, at the age of fifty.

Putting off something until "next year" can be a tricky gambit. It lulls you into a false sense of security, giving you the feeling that you've got plenty of time to get around to it, but not so much time that it'll never happen. The problem with "next year" is that it's always 365 days away. Near, but not yet.

Of course, "soon" is just as dangerous. "Soon" implies a sense of urgent priority but leaves the door open for procrastination. After all, if you don't get to it today, there's always tomorrow, which is still pretty soon.

If something is important enough to do next year, there's a good chance it's important enough to begin right now. And if a year is an appropriate timetable, then attach a date to your goal. The date serves as an anchor in time that brings the goal closer to you every single day. Without a date, "next year" is a dinghy that aimlessly drifts along, endlessly out of reach.

"Tomorrow," "soon," and "next year" may seem like they're just around the corner, but sometimes they're not.

I remember the first time I took my kids to Wrigley Field. It was the year after the Cubs won the World Series, and the kids were excited to see their favorite players in person. It was a beautiful day, the Cubbies won, and we relished singing "Go, Cubs, Go" with forty thousand fellow Cubs fans. It was a first we'll remember forever.

We looked forward to that game for months, as we do for many of the firsts in our lives. Like our first kiss. The first time driving by ourselves. The first place of our own. Our first child.

We prepare for the firsts and anticipate them with the excitement of a little kid on Christmas Eve.

The last times have a habit of sneaking up on us, though.

In our kitchen we have a digital frame that rotates through family photographs. I find myself regularly spying an old snapshot of one of my kids and thinking,

"She was never that little, was she?" Undoubtedly, there was a last time that I held my youngest daughter in the middle of the night, in a grouchy sleep-deprived state, comforting her—begging her—back to sleep. But I don't remember it because when it happened, I didn't realize it was the last time.

The first times come with a lot of fanfare. But the last times come and go without a whisper.

But what if you knew the numbers? Would that change anything?

How many dinners do you have left with your parents?

How many anniversaries do you have left with your spouse?

How many bedtime stories do you have left to read to your kids?

How many fishing trips do you have left with your grandchildren?

How many licks?

There is no machine we can build that will tell us. Not exactly.

We can guess, we can estimate, we can hope for the best.

But I bet that number is a lot smaller than we think it is.

Live accordingly.

"look at everything as though you were seeing it for the first time or the last time. then your time on earth will be filled with glory.

–Betty Smith

the peach that transcends all understanding

Messes and Memories

Eating a peach, in season, perfectly ripe, is pure magic.

But also messy.

Oh, sure, you can eat peaches before they're ripe and they might drip less, but they're not nearly as good. The best peaches are always messy.

Now I'll admit it: I prefer tidy. I like the structure of a good plan. I feel good when the dishes are done and the counter is cleared. I'm easily disturbed when piles stay piles for too long.

Is that an Adultitis-fueled trait? Perhaps. But I do find that I am more present, relaxed, and creative when clutter and chaos are minimized. In general, I don't think it's a terrible trait to have. And I don't believe that an Adultitis-free life is one that disregards any sense of order.

But I still remember the day we let our oldest daughter take control of her own ice cream cone for the first time. It was a beautiful Madison summer afternoon and we were hanging out at the Memorial Union, overlooking picturesque Lake Mendota. We braved the super-duper-long line for ice cream and figured that rather than micromanage each lick, we'd give Lucy full reign over her Zanzibar Chocolate ice cream cone.

Kim handed it to her, and she gave a look of surprise and wonderment that appeared to say, "Are you serious?"

After getting assurance that she was on her own, Lucy dove right in, her hazel eyes shining with joy. She licked. She smiled. She concentrated. She beamed. And she ended up with the cutest brown goatee I ever did see.

Eventually, a tourist from Asia came over and asked permission to take a photo of Lucy. Apparently, the spectacle was of international interest.

Meanwhile, the chocolate mess invaded everywhere from her nose to her toes. Her shirt and shorts were stained. The real breakthrough came when Kim, seeing the mammoth mess unfold before her very eyes, resisted every ounce of motherly urge to wrestle the cone back from our daughter. She let go of the dirty shirt, the sticky fingers, and the crazy sugar buzz that would be left behind.

She let it all go.

Later, she coined a great saying:

Never let making a mess get in the way of making a memory.

I would like to offer a moment of silence for Lucy's tank top. Several washes and stain-stick treatments later, it was unable to be revived and ended up in the trash bin of history. That's okay, though; we've decided that we'd much rather have the memories of that moment than the shirt.

Memories like these are waiting in the wings all the time.

A fan named Jean once wrote to me, "When I see a mud puddle, I step around it. I see muddy shoes and dirty carpets. My kids sit in it. They see dams to build, rivers to cross, and worms to play with." I think we need to take a cue from kids and see the messes in our lives in a new light.

Sometimes budgets get blown and well-made plans go poof.

Sometimes grass stains are inevitable and torn jeans are unavoidable.

Sometimes eggs get broken, milk gets spilled, and the kitchen gets dusted in a fine layer of flour.

Sometimes a scaled-down replica of the Wisconsin State Fair takes over an entire bedroom for several days.

Sometimes life doesn't go the way we planned, expected, or even hoped.

The most direct route is rarely the most scenic, and sometimes wrong turns can lead to the best discoveries.

Adventures are rarely tidy.

Sometimes the best memories arise from the biggest messes.

The Reason for Stonehenge

I remember the painting critiques back in art school. After spending several weeks working on our masterpieces, we'd all sit in a circle and explain what our paintings were about. Someone would inevitably say their piece was a postmodern reaction to the psychological impact of the Industrial Revolution, which caused existential dread. To me, it looked like a canvas with some paint sloppily applied. It did seem like the students who were better at making "serious" art got better grades. (Or perhaps they were just better at explaining why their art was serious.)

Perhaps this is why, after making this painting of Stonehenge constructed with ice cream sandwiches, I feel obliged to explain why.

There are many theories about what Stonehenge is, who built it, when it was built, and what purpose it served. Many theories, but nobody knows for sure.

Of course, someone put it there. *Someone* had a reason for it.

Most theories assume that it served some sort of serious purpose concerning astrological events or burial rituals. But maybe it was simply a good challenge that helped pass the time because nobody had invented cable yet. Maybe it was a primitive tourist attraction. Maybe it was just for fun.

People flock to Stonehenge not because they know what purpose it served, but because of the mystery. And mystery is fun. Plus, Stonehenge looks cool. Which is also fun.

Whimsy and fun are often seen as extras, nonessential. But fun is its own reason for being.

Imagine having the opportunity to jump into a pool of noodles. No child would ever wait until they could answer the question, "What purpose does this serve?"

People with Adultitis need data and statistics before they can justify having fun. Reasons can be found, but if you ask me, most of them are common sense.

Employees who are having fun are happier and do better work.

Customers who are having fun spend more money.

Leaders who are having fun attract more followers.

These are theories that explain why we should take fun seriously. Why not have fun simply because it's fun?

We are constantly in the pursuit of happiness. I don't know about you, but I've never seen someone having fun who is unhappy. Do we really need data to prove that a life filled with fun is better than one that isn't?

Why did those ancient people build Stonehenge? I don't know.

Why did I paint Stonehenge made out of ice cream sandwiches? Because I thought it would be fun.

Sometimes that's the only reason you need.

Why So Serious?

One of the standout lines in the Batman movie *The Dark Knight* comes from Heath Ledger's villainous Joker, who says, "Why so serious?"

The same question might be asked of us.

I remember standing at the bus stop as a young boy, waiting for my early morning ride to school. My mom made me walk the three blocks to the corner much earlier than was necessary, probably ensuring that she wouldn't have to disrupt her morning routine in order to drive her dillydallying son to school.

This meant I had a lot of time on my hands.

One thing that passed the time quite well was playing with maple tree seeds—the blade-shaped fruit that mimics the action of a helicopter as it falls to the ground. What fun it was to grab a handful of seeds, toss them in the air, and watch them spin down around me in a whirling frenzy. They played the military aircraft to my King Kong.

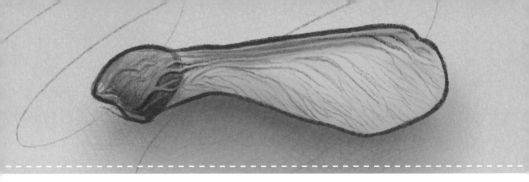

I was reminded of these little guys today on my morning walk. I was on a corner, ready to cross the street, when a single seed spun past my shoulder.

I smiled. I remembered.

Then I thought of God, who originated the design for this diminutive seed: a deceptively simple and seemingly insignificant object of mirth which descends to earth from on high in a clumsy sort of poetic grace.

And then I thought of us humans—particularly the grownup faction—and how we've gotten so adept at making mountains out of molehills. We've mastered the ability of making the trivial monumental. We fret about all sorts of things, from how much gas costs to how we're going to kill those weeds in the yard to what we should wear to next Friday's function. We elevate inconsequential issues to a level of supreme importance.

In the big scheme of things, most of the things that we worry about never happen, and most of the rest don't matter.

Fast-forward thirty-some years to this painting of a pirate ship sailing in an ocean of milk amidst floating Cap'n Crunch cereal. I thought long and hard about conjuring up some deep meaning for this one. Something that would make you nod in amazement and say, "Wow. He is a truly brilliant thinker and artist."

But you know what? There isn't any deep meaning. The truth is, I was thinking about Cap'n Crunch cereal, which I love, and thought about a tiny pirate ship sailing in a bowl of it, which would be neat. But then I thought, what if the ship was normal sized and the whole ocean was milk and it had giant pieces of Cap'n Crunch floating in it? That would be even weirder, and possibly neater.

So that's what I did—gave myself over to pure whimsy.

I have long admired people like Dr. Seuss and Roald Dahl because they created magical characters and worlds that are rich with whimsy. Their art depicts preposterous, physics-bending, imagination-stirring images and scenarios that exhibit a ridiculousness that is wholly original and entertaining. How did they do that? It's hard for me to give myself over to this pure, unadulterated nonsense, which I consider to be the unfiltered essence of the spirit of childhood. I have always wished I could be more like them because I tend to err on the side of practicality and reason. Even as a kid, I was an old soul, so I'm not sure if I have ever experienced this level of creative abandon.

And yet here I am, having created a painting that exists on the same planet, if not at least in the same universe, and I am frustrated because I cannot come up with words to explain the meaning of this painting.

Because there isn't one.

And finally, thankfully, I think, "Well, finally. Some progress."

I'm sure there are plenty of good scientific reasons God designed the maple seed the way He did. But to watch it float to the ground in a perfect display of whimsical silliness makes me wonder; maybe one of the purposes of this design was to whisper a question to anyone who happens to see a maple seed twirling downward. A simple three-word question:

Why so serious?

"while being young is an accident of time, youth is a permanent state of mind.

–Frank Lloyd Wright (*Who was still designing houses when he died at age 91.*)

i'll stop the WORLD and melt with you

Make Someone Happy

This painting was inspired by the lyric of a catchy tune from the '80s by a band named Modern English. Many listeners may not realize that this seemingly simple upbeat love song is actually about the end of the world. Lead singer Robbie Grey, who wrote the song with his four bandmates, explained, "I don't think many people realized it was about a couple making love as the bomb dropped. As they make love, they become one and melt together."

Allllrighty then.

On to another fun fact: This was the very first canvas I painted live during the first ever Madison Night Market. It was also the first time I offered my art for sale to an audience that hadn't just heard me speak. Previously, I'd only sold my art at my speaking engagements, after spending an hour sharing my art on a big screen and telling stories to a captive audience. But here, my art would be standing on its own. No explanation. No context.

As I painted away, I was able to hear people's reactions to the painting and the prints we had for sale. What I heard was magic. People smiled and laughed and pulled their friends over to take a look.

Quite simply, my art made people happy. And that made me feel awesome. I concluded right then and there that if that's all I was ever able to accomplish, it was a worthy calling and it would be enough.

This is kind of a big deal because, you see, in the art world, it's not enough. An artist is supposed to make a political statement, disturb people, or question everything they hold true. Which is fine, as far as it goes. But putting good into the world, making someone happy, and bringing a small measure of joy to a fellow human being is pretty good too.

Which brings me back to this song about apocalyptic hanky-panky.

It seems that every generation fears it's living in the last days. And so far, every one has been wrong. (It remains to be seen how this one fares.) While we wait to see if the world is going to end, let's do something productive with our time. Rioting in the streets, cowering in fear in front of our TVs, and ranting on social media don't seem like good options to me.

Instead, what's ONE thing you can do today to make someone's day just a teeny bit brighter? How can you use one of your gifts to make someone happy? It might not seem like much, but it's enough.

Regardless of when the world ends, we all have a last day coming. I can't say for certain that I'll spend it in the fashion described in the aforementioned '80s song. But if I can make someone happy on my last day (and on many of the days between now and then), I'm good with that.

How about you?

Raspberries to Ya

My grandmother made German cookies called *lebkuchen*, referred to her couch as a "davenport," and hated when her grandkids wore their hats backwards. "Makes you look like hooligans," she'd say. She was also famous for saying, "Raspberries to ya!" I'm pretty sure this witty comeback was a polite (yet colorful) alternative to saying, "Screw you."

So that's where this art came from, painted on the top of a grocery store flyer. At first glance, it appears to be a negative departure from my more optimistic work. But it's negative only in a certain context.

There comes a point in our lives when rolling with the punches doesn't cut it. Sometimes you need to punch back. Not always in a literal sense, of course, but in a way that shows the world the strength that lies within you and shows that you're not backing down.

To all of the setbacks you've experienced on this long road: *Raspberries to ya.*

To that mountain of debt that's enslaved you long enough: *Raspberries to ya.*

To that idiot boss and the soul-crushing job you never liked anyway: *Raspberries to ya.*

To the doubters who said you'll never make it: *Raspberries to ya.*

To the cynics who swear it can't be done: *Raspberries to ya.*

To the critics who've never even stepped foot in the arena: *Raspberries to ya.*

To Adultitis, its unadventurous version of adulthood, and all its stupid rules: *Raspberries to ya.*

When used in reply to setbacks and cynics, curmudgeons and critics, this humble piece of artwork suddenly becomes downright empowering.

Keep fighting.

the art of being wise is the art of knowing what to overlook.

–William James

Shine On

After months of anticipation about our family's first trip to Mexico and an escape from the Wisconsin winter, the weather report turned foreboding. All eight days were calling for rain. Kim and I were crushed. Our family had finally recovered from a three-week battle with the flu over the holidays, and we were looking forward to the time away to recharge in the sun and surf. Kim was especially fretful about the forecast of rain, incessantly checking the weather app on her phone.

On the plane, I read a section in a devotional about God being a "living God." That struck me. I grew up thinking of God as some far-off historical figure who did a lot of neat things in olden times, forgetting that He lives in the present tense, active in the here and now.

In that moment, I felt totally at peace. Did I expect God to alter a weather system on account of li'l old us? To be honest, I guess I hoped He would, but more than that, I knew that the only way to really ruin the vacation was to spend all our time worried and anxious over the weather report. Even if it rained the whole trip, we would still have an opportunity to be together and to rest, away from the hustle and bustle of our daily lives.

We did pray for sunshine, but we also prayed for peace to melt away our fears, and for the perspective to make the best of whatever each day would bring.

No one knows with certainty what next year, next week, or even what tomorrow will bring. (Not me, not you, and certainly not weather forecasters!) But too often in life, we allow doubt and anxiety to dominate our perspective, and we live out our fears in advance. I knew that God knew how big of a deal this trip was to us, and He would give us what we needed from it, even if it didn't look exactly how we imagined it.

So here's what happened. Every single evening, the weather app on our phones indicated storms for the next day. And every single day, we woke up to sunny skies, while the thundercloud icon had vanished. The only rain we experienced was about a half-hour's worth on our last day, and it came as a welcome relief during a hot walk at the Tulum ruins.

The abundant sunshine became a symbol to us of God's goodness. As the trip was coming to an end, we searched for a sunshine-themed souvenir to bring home with us, something to remind ourselves of what felt like a mini-miracle and God's active presence in our lives. We never did find anything just right.

We arrived home at about midnight. Our youngest child was asleep as we pulled into our driveway. A few police officers were canvassing the street with flashlights, clearly looking for something. We didn't think much of it, figuring the neighbor kid was in trouble again.

As our tired bodies, carrying overfilled suitcases, stumbled into the house, our oldest daughter said, "Hey, what's that on the ceiling?" I looked up and saw a gash in the drywall. The directional groove led my eye to the window, which had a bullet hole in it.

A bullet hole.

"Kim," I said, "Hurry and go tell the cops that we have a bullet hole in our window!"

The rest of the evening was a blur. We found small bits of glass all over the carpet and on the piano across the room. The officers pulled a bullet fragment from the ceiling, but it was too mangled to be of any use. They had very little information for us, except for the reports from neighbors, who had heard multiple gunshots and a speeding car with a bad muffler. At first, I was annoyed that I had to postpone the date with my bed to deal with this after having had an awesome vacation, but eventually, it hit me. *Wait. What if we had been home? This bullet could have hit one of my kids.*

The mood quickly turned from annoyance to anger and fear.

None of us got much sleep that night. (Except Ginny, who was already asleep and would ask about that taped-up cardboard patch on our window two whole days later.)

The next morning, our six-year-old son, Ben, brought a bullet to Kim that he found in the hallway. "Momma, what's this?" he asked.

Another call to the police.

The next few weeks were a blur of logistics and emotion. Assurances from the police that our neighborhood was historically among the safest in the city didn't seem to help. Calls to the insurance company and various vendors about replacing the window and fixing the damaged ceiling were interspersed with the feeling of being violated and wondering if we were still in danger. I'd never seen my wife cry so much in all of our eighteen years of marriage.

We heard stories from neighbors who'd been home. Three young girls next door were in the front room watching TV when the shooting happened. An elderly neighbor across the street told us the gunshots were so loud that she thought her house was the one under attack. A young mother in the home next to hers was nursing her two-month-old in her front room. She hit the deck when the shots rang out. Everyone was shaken. For days, we saw cars slow down in front of our house to gawk at the scene of the crime.

Eventually, amidst the haze of fear and confusion, we began to notice where

God had been working in the situation.

We realized that our house was the only one on the whole block that was empty when the shooting occurred. We figured out that it wouldn't have been had we not been held up in Minneapolis so our plane could be de-iced. We felt His presence in the neighborhood meeting that was organized two days after the incident. Over fifty people crammed into a basement owned by a former police officer, bonding together to comfort one another and talk about practical ways to protect our neighborhood. It was neat to see connections get made and friendships deepen.

Finally, Kim and I got to a place where we could ask, "What does this terrible event make possible?"

Years earlier, we had stayed in a vacation home in Santa Barbara that featured some stained-glass windows. We'd always been smitten by their charm, so we wondered if we could replace the broken front window in our living room with a stained-glass work of art. The fact that the window in question was a decorative half-circle above the normal windows made it a perfect candidate. Maybe I could even design it. And maybe it would give hope to the rest of the neighborhood. We knew immediately what the design had to be.

A sun.

We got connected with the guy who created the stained-glass windows at our church, and I gave him a sketch. We got our sunshine souvenir after all—after we returned home and in a form we never anticipated. It now serves as a beacon of hope to the entire neighborhood.

We live in a dark world, where tragedy and pain are all too common. Sometimes vacations do get rained out. Sometimes bullets don't miss. But I believe this: God is a living God. He gives us small signs—signs that don't seem like much in the grand scheme of things—just to let us know He is there. I think the reason He does this is so that when the bad things happen, we'll remember that He is still there, ready to bring good things out of terrible circumstances. He gives us the sunny days to recharge us, to fill our reserves with hope that lights the way during the dark times, reminding us that the sun will shine again.

It's worth remembering that even on the darkest, cloudiest days, the sun doesn't disappear. It's still there; it's just hidden. The people who see silver linings are the ones who look for them. If you are in a dark season right now, keep looking for the light. It's coming.

Finally, I believe we are called to be a light for others. We do this by sharing our gifts and by being kind. When it comes to people who disagree with us, instead of calling them names, we can call them up for coffee. The smallest things can make the biggest difference. Our happiness increases when we help others, shining our own lights outward.

In the battle between light and darkness, the darkness doesn't stand a chance.

Shine on.

Enjoy the Ride

This painting was inspired by the aforementioned trip to Mexico, the beautiful tradition of *Dia de Muertos*, and thoughts of loved ones who have come before.

Life can seem like such a slog sometimes. A constant struggle of trying to get ahead, putting out fires, overcoming one obstacle after another. Sometimes we're simply in survival mode, and it takes everything we've got just to make it through the day. It's easy to grow tired and become discouraged, maybe even bitter and a little angry.

This is because we don't have perspective.

Our ancestors, who have already traversed this lifespan and have seen what's beyond, have a different perspective than we do. They are now able to see the big picture. They went through the valleys, but the blessings that came out of those sojourns were ultimately revealed. Our ancestors have the full understanding that the journey is shorter than we realize. Like us, they experienced darkness, but they have received the gift of perspective that allows them to see the beauty in it all.

If the loved ones who have gone before us could give us advice, it might just be this: *enjoy the ride.*

In this book, I've written about a flooded basement, a ruined painting, and a broken window. In the grand scheme of life, these are not tragedies worthy of being featured in a disaster movie by James Cameron.

I have a friend who lost his eyesight in his twenties. Another friend became paralyzed in a farm accident, and yet another lost a leg to cancer when he was a kid. Events like these are indeed life-changing, but they are also rare.

The other kind—the roadblocks, the setbacks, the molehills disguised as mountains—pop up all the time. How we approach these more common events matters, because how we choose to perceive them can be just as life-changing.

Norman Vincent Peale wrote, "Problems can be good for you, although they may be painful at the time. All worthwhile achievements are the result of problem solving. When I hear some troubled person cry, 'Why does God let this happen to me?' I often feel like saying, 'Because He knows you'll grow and be strengthened if you grapple with your difficulty.'"

Problems are opportunities. So are failed plans. Ruined basements. Torn canvases. And bullet-ridden window panes.

Changing the way we see really can change everything.

The rain will come, but the sunshine is always sure to follow. No matter how dire our straits or how difficult life becomes, with a little faith and new eyes, we can always expect a 100 percent chance of awesome.

You just need to look for it.

the sky is not less blue
because a blind man
does not see it.

–Danish proverb

Questions to Ponder

I hope this book has shed some new light into your life. In the following pages,
I've included some questions inspired by each chapter to help you take things
to the next level. They're perfect for individual reflection and journaling, but
can also be great conversation starters for book clubs and discussion groups.
I've also created a customized set of questions for teams and organizations
to use on retreats and in staff meetings to help them become more innovative,
productive, and profitable. You can find them at **aChanceOfAwesome.com**

Need lots of books? We can give you a good deal!
Contact store@escapeadulthood.com for details.

Weeds or Wishes (p. 1)

Where is Adultitis wreaking the most havoc in your life right now? What's one thing you could do help start to turn the tide?

a 100% Chance of Awesome (p. 5)

What is something frustrating or unexpected that has happened in your life recently that is the best candidate to be a "happy accident?"

See With New Eyes (p. 11)

Do you consider yourself a person who is more near-sighted or one who is more far-sighted? When has that trait been helpful, and when has it been a hindrance?

Looking for Orcas (p. 17)

When in your life did you get something you wanted, even though at first it didn't look like it at the time?

Space Invaders (p. 21)

Think of something frustrating you right now. How can you make dealing with it or overcoming it into a game?

Get Up Faster (p. 25)

Where in your life right now is there an opportunity to get up faster?

Enjoy the Woo (p. 33)

Even if you don't believe they'll happen, come up with three potential best-case scenarios for something in your life that you currently feel anxious about.

Bee Optimistic (p. 37)

What's one thing you could do to encourage someone else who is currently fighting a hard battle?

Mind Your Own Monkeys (p. 45)

Think of the most difficult person in your life. After reading this chapter, what plan of action seems to make the most sense in dealing with this individual going forward?

Duck Duck Goose (p. 51)

What is one practical way you can create more time for solitude in your life?

Willing to Relocate (p. 57)

Where are you settling in your life right now? What is an area in your life that might benefit from a relocation?

Draw Upside Down (p. 61)

Who is someone you could swap roles with this week that will help you both gain a new perspective?

Art vs. Science

Do you see yourself more as an Artist or a Scientist? What is something you could try to incorporate a strength often associated with the other?

This Ain't Kansas

What is one routine you can upend this week?

Best Practices Are for the Birds

What area of your life feels a little bit too much like a "paint-by-number?" What is something you can do to add a little creativity?

Hippoposterous

What's your biggest dream that feels preposterous? Instead of telling yourself "No," tell yourself, "Yes, if..." Now, follow up that "if" with what would be required to make your dream possible.

The Invasion of Nonsense

What is the biggest challenge you are dealing with right now? Make a list of ten ridiculous solutions to that problem. After you've made the list, examine your answers for one clue that prompts a doable next step that might be worth trying.

More Cowbell Please

What unused talent, discarded fixer-upper, or lost cause in your life has the potential to be an opportunity hidden in plain sight?

The Good Old Days (p. 99)

Think of three good things in your life right now that will not last forever. What will you do this week to make the most of them?

Half Full (p. 109)

What's something good that ended up coming from a failure you experienced in your life?

Doughnuts and Optimism (p. 115)

Think of something you are currently struggling with or worried about. What are five good things that might arise from this experience?

Must Be Nice (p. 119)

What are three of your "must be nices" (strengths, talents, natural advantages)? How could you utilize them even better than you currently are?

How to Be Lucky (p. 125)

What is one thing you can do this month to get better at something you're already pretty good at?

The Night Light (p. 129)

What is your biggest fear or concern right now? Spend some time writing out answers to the following questions: What is the worst-case scenario you can imagine? What is the absolute best-case scenario? What is most likely to happen in this scenario?

What if it Works? (p. 137)

What initiative have you recently begun or are thinking about undertaking that's freaking you out a little bit? What are five awesome things that could happen if everything goes well?

Not Sunk Yet (p. 141)

What is something positive you can begin this week that you will be happy you did one year from now?

Ready for Lift-Off (p. 145)

What is something you're currently trying to accomplish that's become more difficult or taking longer than you thought it would? After reminding yourself that it's OK (and probably normal), what's one positive thing – no matter how small – that has happened since you've begun?

Keep On Fishing (p. 149)

Where do you feel like you've hit a dead-end? What is something you haven't tried in a while that might be worth trying again, or in a slightly different way? Who is someone you could talk to that might give you a new idea to explore?

Pie in the Sky (p. 153)

Where do the odds feel stacked against you? What does the situation have to look like before you're willing to throw in the towel? If you're not there yet, keep going. If you are, it's OK to move on and try something new. But you have to decide.

Wind In Our Sails (p. 157)

Who are five people that have served as wind in your sails? What can you do to honor them in some way to show your appreciation?

Look for Miracles (p. 161)

What failure, dead end, or disappointment that you're currently experiencing is the best candidate for becoming the foundation of something awesome?

What is Beautiful (p. 167)

Make a list of things that make you happy. What's something you can do to incorporate more of that into your life?

How Many Licks? (p. 171)

Is there something you've always wanted to do that you keep putting off? Is there anything you're putting off that could be accomplished in the next month with a little effort? What are you waiting for?

Messes and Memories (p. 179)

What relationship or area of your life could benefit from a willingness on your part to put up with a little messiness?

The Reason for Stonehenge (p. 185)

What's one thing you can do to make some element of your life (a relationship, a dreaded routine, your wardrobe, commute or voicemail message) more fun?

Why So Serious? (p. 189)

What is one aspect of your life that could benefit from a little less seriousness?

Make Someone Happy (p. 195)

What's one thing you can do to make someone else's day a teeny bit brighter today?

Raspberries to Ya (p. 199)

What person, group, policy, or self-limiting belief is it time for you to start ignoring or let go of?

Shine On (p. 203)

What dark cloud has recently rolled into your life? What does it make possible?

Enjoy the Ride (p. 211)

What is the one challenge, situation or relationship in your life that would benefit the most from a change in your perspective?

ESCAPE
ADULTHOOD

Drop Jason a line at
jason@escapeadulthood.com

For a treasure trove of Adultitis-fighting tips & tools,
or to learn more about bringing in Jason to speak
to your organization, skedaddle on over to
escapeadulthood.com

jason kotecki is a professional reminder-er and permission granter who moonlights as an artist, author and professional speaker. Jason and his wife Kim have made it their mission in life to help people and organizations break free from Adultitis to build better lives, businesses, and teams.

Jason has written seven books, and his colorful art has been collected and licensed all over the world. As a speaker, Jason works with organizations to beat burnout and become more innovative by breaking rules that don't exist. His content-rich programs are balanced with a refreshing mix of humor and emotion, serving as the perfect antidote for people who find themselves in a personal or professional rut.

Ultimately, Jason creates art, observations, and experiences that give people hope and the freedom to live joyfully. His greatest desire is to use his talents to share God's love and impact lives by inspiring, entertaining and encouraging people to rekindle their childlike spirit and create the lives they were made for.

An avid eater of sugar-laden cereal, Jason enjoys Star Wars, soft t-shirts, and brand new tubes of paint. He and Kim homeschool their three weird kids and live in Madison, Wisconsin where they eat way too many cheese curds.

Is there a particular piece of art from this book that you just loved? Jason's art has been collected by fans all over the world. Browse the Lemonade Stand for a wide selection of prints, greeting cards, t-shirts, originals and other goodies featuring your favorite work from Jason!

Visit EscapeAdulthood.com/shop

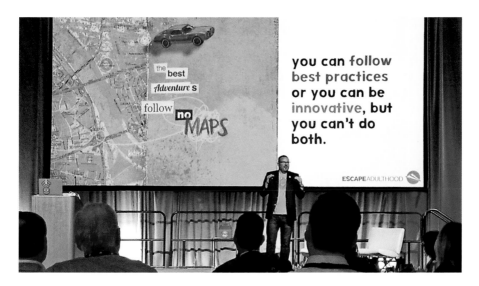

A sought-after keynote speaker, Jason has been hired by some of the world's largest organizations looking to increase morale, engagement, and innovative thinking. Recognized as a Certified Speaking Professional® by the National Speakers Association (a designation held by only 10% of speakers in the world), Jason's message reaches tens of thousands of people each year. His inspiring, engaging, and heart-warming programs are visual masterpieces jam-packed with relevant, practical information coated in fun that help people become more passionate, productive, and profitable.

Learn more at EscapeAdulthood.com/speaking

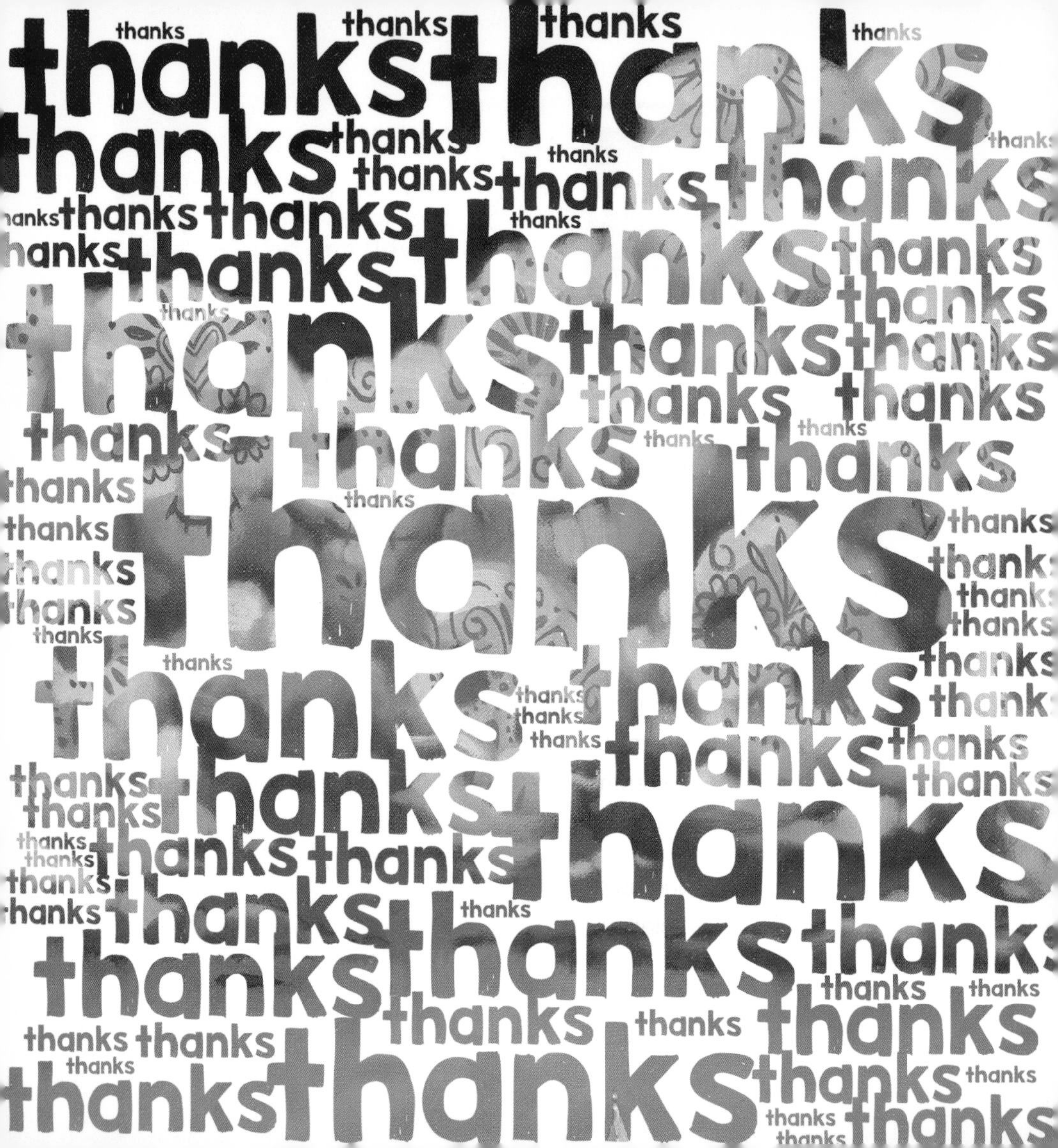
thanks

Many Thanks

Of course, this book would not exist without the tremendous amount of support, encouragement and counsel I have received from so many kind and generous people.

First of all, I offer my appreciation to you, dear reader, for taking the time to read this weird book that doesn't quite fit into the box of what a book for grown-ups is supposed to be.

To the merry band of Adultitis Fighters that has rallied around this noble cause, and anyone who has ever read my words, purchased my art, or booked me to speak, your kind feedback and enthusiasm brightens my life, serves as fuel, and lets me know that my work matters.

Catherine, your sharp eyes and hard questions helped me re-examine my beliefs, express myself more clearly, and made this book so much better.

To Mom and Dad, thank you for believing this art thing was worth pursuing. And for buying me more than my fair share of eyeglasses.

To my brothers, for supporting my big dreams while making sure my head doesn't follow suit.

To Gary and Joyce, for your prayers, example, and allowing your daughter to marry an artist.

To Sue and Jenna, the steadfast companions who have supported me along every stretch of this epic roller coaster.

To Lucy, Ben, and Ginny, you've always been my biggest inspiration, but you're growing into my biggest cheerleaders. I'm so proud to be your dad.

To Kim, my soul-mate, my sounding board, and my partner in crime. Thank you for the smiles, support, and shenanigans you bring into my life. I don't make sense. You don't make sense. But somehow, together, we make sense.

Finally, I second what the great composer Bach inscribed at the end of each of his compositions: **Soli Deo Gloria**

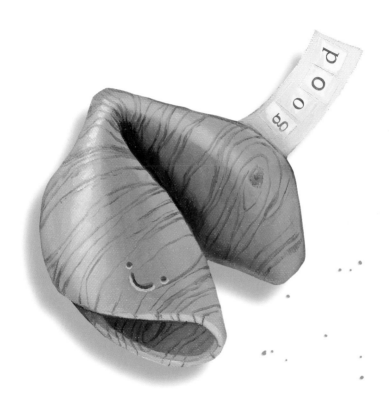

time for awesome